Year 1

Disciples

follow me
Daily Readings for Disciples

By Peter Slofstra and Peter Schuurman

FAITH
ALIVE.
Christian Resources

Follow Me: Daily Readings for Disciples, © 2007 by Faith Alive Christian Resources, 2850 Kalamazoo Ave. SE, Grand Rapids, MI 49560. All rights reserved. With the exception of brief excerpts for review purposes, no part of this book may be reproduced in any manner whatsoever without written permission from the publisher. Printed in the United States of America on recycled paper.

This book is part of Disciples, a comprehensive multi-year faith formation program for adults.

We welcome your comments. Call us at 1-800-333-8300 or e-mail us at editors@faithaliveresources.org.

Library of Congress Cataloging-in-Publication Data

Slofstra, Peter.
  Follow me: daily readings for disciples / by Peter Slofstra and Peter Schuurman.
     p. cm.
  ISBN-13: 978-1-59255-401-0 (alk. paper)
  1. Meditations. 2. Christian life—Christian Reformed authors. I. Schuurman, Peter. II. Title.
  BV4832.3S56 2007
  242'.2—dc22
                              2007003931

10 9 8 7 6 5 4 3 2 1

Contents

Authors

We both believe God has a tremendous sense of humor. That we, with the help of our wives, are writing a book of daily devotional readings together is a hilarious thing.

Let us explain. Although separated by almost two decades in age, we not only have the same first name and initials, but we both grew up in Willowdale, Ontario, and attended the Christian Reformed church there. Similarly, we both lived for some time in New Westminster, British Columbia; Grand Rapids, Michigan; and St. Catharines, Ontario, where we actually met and were a part of Jubilee Fellowship.

We do have different jobs. 2 Peter now lives in Guelph. He's employed by CRC Home Missions to build up campus ministries in North America.

1 Peter, as far as we know, has no plans to move to Guelph. He is pastor at Hope Fellowship in Courtice, Ontario, right next to Oshawa. That's the town where 2 Peter was born.

Although we wrote an equal number of these devotions, we decided not to reveal which ones were done by whom. We want to leave it a mystery—or you can guess who the "I" is as you go.

—Peter Slofstra and Peter Schuurman

Pause

We live in a fast-paced world that places high value on speed, productivity, and efficiency. If we are honest, sometimes we measure our discipleship by the same values. We want results!

What if discipleship were first and foremost a beautiful journey? What if we believed our relationship with God was the most beautiful personal encounter we've ever had? What if we deeply desired to pattern our lives after this awesome tenderness we know as grace?

We hope our meditations give you opportunity to stop and ask the big questions. Not so much the big philosophical questions but the big questions about whom you follow, who you are, and how you are going to live. Because at the end of your life, will you and your loved ones focus on how successful or impressive your life was, or on how beautiful it became as you grew towards maturity in Christ?

We believe nothing is more beautiful than God. The evidence is all around us. Our desire is to live more deeply into the life and heart of God.

We hope these ponderings on the Bible help along the way.

Necklace 1

> *"We are God's work of art, created*
> *in Christ Jesus to live the good life*
> *as from the beginning*
> *he had meant us to live it."*
>
> —Ephesians 2:10, Jerusalem Bible

"Beautiful cross, man," said this long-haired youth to me. "Sweet."

I stopped, looked down at the small metal ornament around my neck. I had forgotten I was wearing it. It was just one horizontal metal line imposed over a vertical metal line. Simple but elegant. I suppose you could call it beautiful.

Yet if you think about the history of this design, it is anything but beautiful. The cross was originally a method of torture and execution, intended to produce an excruciating death for its victim. It was a tool of oppressive empires, a method of murder that would frighten potentially revolutionary hearts, intimidating all who would witness its wicked work. It is a bloody, ugly symbol.

What happened to change this association?

Over two thousand years ago a man named Jesus deliberately allowed himself to be arrested, accused, tortured, and executed on a cross in order to demonstrate to the world that the power of love is greater than the love of power. On the cross he absorbed

all the hate and violence of human and superhuman powers (we'll call it "the empire"), and transformed them into a divine, death-defying power: sacrificial love. What the empire intended for evil on the cross, Jesus turned into good as he rose from his execution to demonstrate the power of love.

The focus of this set of devotions is discipleship. Not just any discipleship, but discipleship in the footsteps of Jesus, who is called The Christ. It involves not just believing in him, not just identifying with him, but following him into the darkest places he journeys. We do so not because it's the rational thing to do, or because we have tried out all the other options on the religious market. Strange as it may seem, this journey with Jesus is the most beautiful thing we can do with our lives. Paul says that God in his grace is making us into "works of art" (or literally from the Greek, *poems*) intended for the good of the world.

To be a disciple of Jesus is to participate in God's beautiful transforming energy. It is to be part of a revolutionary movement that revolutionizes what revolutions have always been about. With Jesus, swords are beaten into plowshares (see Joel 3:10) and the cross of torture is changed into a cross of peace. It's a beautiful cross because of this beautiful transformation.

The movie *La Vita E Bella (Life Is Beautiful)* gives us a picture of what beautiful discipleship might mean. In this film, Guido, a man full of life, laughter, and love is arrested and taken with his family to a concentration camp during World War II. Although he and his son Joshua are surrounded by violence and hate, Guido insists that the culture of cruelty is not the ultimate reality. He constantly explains to his boy that the tragedy unfolding before his eyes is really a comedy, a game that will end with a great prize for the winner—a giant army tank.

On one hand, the viewer knows that the Holocaust is no game, and the daily fare of murder is not pretend. On the other hand, the Christian viewer can agree that the horror and hell of war are not uncontested. Like Guido, our love must lead us to imagine an alternative way of living and a new future. This is the practice of resurrected life.

Today the cross crowns the top of churches and adorns the front of Christian sanctuaries. That single horizontal line has been joined with a vertical line in a multitude of ways—with wood, nails, and spikes; and glass, gold, and jewels. People raise it high in parades, they sing about the love it offers, and it brings tears, not of pain, but of joy. It's a beautiful cross!

The ugly cross has been made beautiful by a beautiful Lord. Ultimately, our focus is not the cross, but the beautiful Savior who made its lowliness his crowning glory. These devotions are an invitation to participate in his beauty and make your life a work of art. They are a call to imagine a world of love, and to conspire toward the good, no matter what powers may shape the world otherwise.

Talk It Over

1. What other organizations use the cross as a symbol, and in what ways do they share some similar goals with disciples of Jesus?

2. Can we distinguish between believers and disciples? What is the difference?

3. Before Jesus' arrest, a woman pours perfume on him. Jesus says "She has done a beautiful thing to me" (Matt. 26:10). Why was her action "beautiful"? What beautiful thing might you do today that could contribute to God's world of love?

In Other Words

What once was hurt
what once was friction
what left a mark
no longer stings . . .
because Grace makes beauty
out of ugly things.

—U2, from "Grace," *All That You Can't Leave Behind*

Do Something!

Make or buy a cross and fashion it into a necklace. Wear it for a week and see how it feels on you. Does it remind you of who you are? What comments arise from others?

Desire 2

> *"Jesus saw them following and asked,*
> *'What do you want?'"*
>
> —John 1:38

In the movie *The Notebook*, based on Nicholas Sparks's tender novel, we meet Allie and Noah, an elderly couple in a nursing home. She is in the grip of Alzheimer's disease. In an attempt to help his wife remember him, Noah spends time every day reading her own journal back to her, the journal that tells the story of how they fell in love and became a couple.

In one of the film's pivotal flashbacks, a younger Allie is torn between her fiancé, Lon Hammond, Jr., who represents a secure future, and a younger Noah Calhoun, who represents passionate love.

Young Noah says: "So it's not gonna be easy. It's gonna be really hard. We're gonna have to work at this every day, but I want to do that because I want you. I want all of you, forever, you and me, every day. Will you do something for me, please? Just picture your life for me? Thirty years from now, forty years from now? What's it look like? If it's with him, go. Go! I lost you once; I think I can do it again. If I thought that's what you really wanted. But don't you take the easy way out."

Allie responds: "What easy way? There is no easy way. No matter what I do, somebody gets hurt."

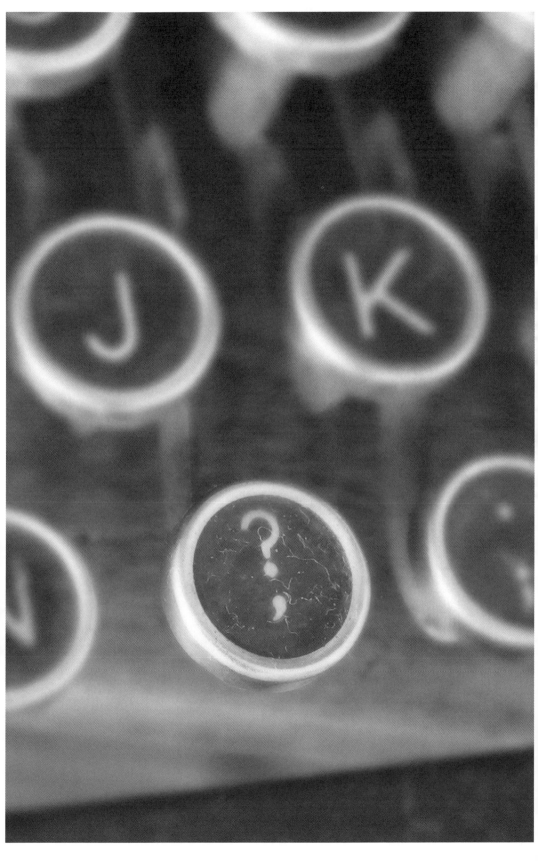

Noah pleads: "Would you stop thinking about what everyone wants? Stop thinking about what I want, what he wants, what your parents want. What do *you* want? What do you *want*?"

Allie cries: "It's not that simple!"

Noah shouts: "WHAT . . . DO . . . YOU . . . WANT? WHADDAYA WANT?"

At that moment Allie could only say, "I have to go now." But after a meeting with her fiancé, she makes her final decision. She chooses Noah. And thirty or forty years later they die in each other's arms in the nursing home where the movie begins.

What helped Allie to decide was the piercing question at the core of everything: "What do you want?" In the gospel of John, those same four words are exactly the first recorded words of the Lord Jesus Christ. They are directed at Andrew at the pivotal moment when he leaves John the Baptist to find out more about this Jesus. And these four words have the same impact, the same importance as they did in *The Notebook.* More impact and more importance, in fact, because Noah and Allie are only fictional characters whereas Jesus and Andrew . . . and you and I . . . are real!

Jesus now asks us: "What do you want?" It's a discipleship question.

In other words, "What do you want from me? What do you want for yourself? How do you picture your life, now and thirty or forty years from now? What are you hoping for, longing for, living for? What do you really want out of life? What will make your life beautiful?"

How did Andrew respond? He asked, "Rabbi, where are you staying?" (John 1:38b) In other words, Can I spend some time there with you? This suggests that he already understood that what really matters in life has less to do with "What" and more to do with "Who."

You probably know that too. Things don't make people happy; relationships do. And as far as relationships are concerned, the most important relationship is with the God who knows us through and through and wants to make us fully alive. When our wants overlap with God's desires, life becomes truly beautiful.

Talk It Over

Saint Ignatius said that discipleship can move through three stages, roughly summarized this way:

"I want what I want the way I want it."
"I want what God wants the way I want it."
"I want what God wants the way he wants it."

Where are you?

How do you discern whether or not your wants and God's desires are in beautiful harmony?

In Other Words

"Why do we hunger for beauty so right?"

—Jim Croegaert, "Why Do We Hunger?" on Steve Bell's CD *Deep Calls to Deep*

Do Something!

The website "43 Things" asks visitors, "What do you want to do with your life?" Make a list of five things that you would love to do with your own life. Share it with your family or small group.

Pattern 3

"The Proverbs of Solomon . . . For acquiring a disciplined and prudent life."

—Prov. 1:3, NRSV

Without personal discipline, you will not improve or grow. This is true for every part of our lives, including school, sports, music, or finances. The maxim "5 percent inspiration, 95 percent perspiration" applies not only to learning a new language or training for a marathon, but also to the disciplines designed to develop your faith, often called "spiritual disciplines."

What are spiritual disciplines? According to Robert Longman, Jr., they are "habits or regular patterns in your life that repeatedly bring you back to God and open you up to what God is saying to you." There are many lists of spiritual disciplines, and we'll be returning to this important aspect of discipleship often in the course of the studies to follow. Here are a few of the basics:

Prayer and Bible reading. Praying is something we can do all day long. But it is also helpful to find a time that works, a place that works, and a plan that works for regular prayer and Bible reading. The Bible is essential, and there are daily devotional books and booklets that open up the Scriptures in fresh ways. In prayer we speak and listen to God in response to the biblical Word.

Public worship. Although worship is not limited to what happens on Sunday mornings, New Testament believers knew that gathering with

God's people for worship, Word, and sacraments was important for personal growth and the well-being of the whole church community. Regular worship also helps us to see our lives from God's perspective. For Jesus' disciples today, church attendance is not a weekly "we'll see how we feel" proposition, but a weekly "good habit"—even on a business trip or vacation.

Small groups. In a small group, believers can interact more personally, share interests and concerns, discuss ideas, go deeper into the Word of God, and pray for each other. There is nothing like a small group to give a sense of belonging and accountability.

Giving. Christians give. They give out of gratitude; they give because of compassion. But this too is a spiritual discipline. And as a discipline, it often needs to be developed. Every Christian would benefit from a money management course based on biblical principles that teaches you not only how to spend, save, and invest wisely, but also how to give generously.

Using your gifts. If you want to grow spiritually, you should discover and use the gifts the Holy Spirit has given you. Stepping into an area of ministry in which God has gifted you forces you to grow in faith. Don't let self-doubt stop you from trying. Get out of your comfort zone. Grow by using your God-given gifts.

Reflection and solitude. Listen to Christian singer-songwriters and reflect on their lyrics. Read books by Christian authors and think about their insights. Go on a silent retreat or register for a conference. Meditate, write a journal, pray and fast. Be still and get on God's wavelength again.

One caution: spiritual disciplines will not save you. Jesus did that. They will not purify you. The Holy Spirit does that. Spiritual disciplines are not "works righteousness" in disguise. They are grateful responses to God's beautiful grace.

So what can spiritual disciplines do? They can help you experience intimacy with God. They can keep you on track when life threatens to blow you off course. They can help you "encourage one another" as fellow travelers on the narrow road. Spiritual disciplines help Christ's disciples hear the Master's voice!

Life is too busy, expectations are too high, and stress is too relentless to neglect the good patterns of the Christian life. You have more choice and more control of your schedule than you may think.

Talk It Over

1. Which spiritual disciplines are you drawn to? Why?

2. In which spiritual disciplines do you want to grow? In which do you need to grow?

3. Give an example of a regular pattern in your life that has encouraged you in your faith or helped you hear the Lord's voice more clearly.

In Other Words

"Kingdom living means choosing deliberate solitude, intentional community, time for prayer, meditation, and fasting. It means living a life of premeditated submission to the people around us and serving them, washing feet like the Master. It's a different way—a redemptive way—of living life in the world, not a way of stepping out of it."

—Dallas Willard, *Spirit of the Disciplines*

Do Something!

Write out your favorite Bible verse on an index card and memorize it this week. Tell someone what it is and why.

Athlete 4

*"Athletes exercise self-control in all things;
they do it to receive a perishable wreath,
but we an imperishable one."*

—1 Corinthians 9:25, NRSV

Every worthwhile accomplishment requires self-discipline. Setting a significant goal is only a first step. An important step, mind you. But it must be backed up not only with a plan but also with the daily discipline to say yes to whatever supports the goal and no to whatever hinders it.

Let's say that one of your personal goals is to enter a local road race. You pick a 5-kilometer race that will be run three months from now. You write it on the calendar. You send in your application. Now what do you do?

My advice would be to download a training schedule from a website about running. Goals need plans. The goal of running a race requires a schedule that tells you how often, how far, and how hard you need to run each week for the twelve weeks leading up to race day.

With the date set and a training schedule taped to the fridge, you have a goal and a plan. Then comes the hard part: the daily discipline of actually doing the required training. Regardless of whether you are a beginning runner who must walk/run for thirty minutes at least three times a week or an advanced runner following a weekly program of speed work, tempo runs, and long runs, you

will have to get out there and do the time and the distance. Your most important exercise will be exercising self-discipline.

It isn't easy. It's one thing to say yes to that 5k race; it's another thing altogether to say no to the snooze button on your alarm, to the fatty snacks that add inches to your waistline, and to the late-night shows that cut minutes from your sleep. But it's incredibly rewarding, especially when that internal voice that told you it's too tiring, cold, wet, or early is finally drowned out by voices at the finish line shouting, "Way to go! You're looking great!"

What's the main difference between those who dream and those who do? Self-discipline. A dream gets you going; self-discipline gets you there.

There are many goals that will only be achieved by living "a disciplined and prudent life." Finishing a race is just one example. Getting an education, paying down a mortgage or paying the rent on time, playing an instrument, and losing weight are other goals that require lots of self-discipline.

The most important goal of all, becoming more like Jesus, requires the most discipline of all. Essentially, disciples of Jesus are spiritual athletes in training to be godly (1 Tim. 4:8). Their training requires them to repeatedly say yes to whatever helps and no to whatever gets in the way of becoming mature in Christ.

We can take heart from the fact that the disciples struggled with self-discipline. James and John, the "sons of thunder," found it hard to control their angry responses to communities that would not welcome Jesus. Peter struggled with thinking before speaking. The apostle Paul complained, "the evil I do not want to do I keep on doing." Clearly, the self is not an easy thing to discipline.

What helped them become more self-disciplined? Several things. They surrendered their wills to Jesus and gave him mastery over their lives. They came together for the purpose of encouraging each other to follow Jesus. And they knew that they could always get back to the starting line because of God's forgiveness.

If you are disappointed in your track record when it comes to reaching your goals, especially the goal of living a life that glorifies God "by doing what is right and just and fair," you may have to take a good hard look at your ability to control your willful self. If self-discipline is a problem, make it a matter of prayer and accountability. Ask the Lord to give you the strength to say yes to whatever is godly and good and no to whatever hinders God's beautiful dreams for you. Make yourself accountable to a person or small group so that you will be challenged and encouraged to stay the course.

Disciples of Jesus are spiritual athletes. Enjoy exercising your spiritual self-discipline to bring glory to God and joy to your life as you "run with perseverance the race marked out for you." (Hebrews 12:1)

Talk It Over

1. What are your goals for your walk with the Lord?

2. How do you plan to accomplish these goals?

3. How would you rate yourself in terms of your self-discipline?

4. What can you do to improve in this area of your life?

In Other Words

"When I run, I feel [God's] pleasure."
—Eric Liddel, 1924, as told in the film *Chariots of Fire*

Do Something!

With some other members of your family, friends, or small group, register for an upcoming walking, running, or cycling event and train for it together.

Clothing 5

"For our struggle is not against flesh and blood, but against the rulers, against the authorities, against the powers of this dark world and against the spiritual forces of evil in the heavenly realms."
—Ephesians 6:12

The heart of discipleship is the hunger for a meaningful life. While this involves gentleness and patience, it is not all sweetness and softness. Discipleship takes place in the context of a war, a war in which powers contend for individual souls and national cultures. To be gentle and patient in this context requires a profound inner strength aided by divinely woven protective clothing—what has been called "the armor of God."

In order to costume ourselves with such armor, we must first take off the outfit that our culture has given us. This is the clothing that equips us to "take care of number one." For example, we will need to take off the belt of good impressions. This is our tendency to focus on image, manipulating our outward appearance and actions to look better than they really are.

Then we need to pull off the checkerboard shirt of compartmentalization. The white squares on it represent our prayer, church, and singing selves. Separating them are the black squares of our

sports, entertainment, and workplace selves. This shirt never fit well anyway, as it was always shifting around.

Although it is difficult, we must unlace the shoes of competition and lay them aside. We will no longer need to get one up on our neighbor and his stuff, or share that little remark about our brother or sister in church that enables us to feel just a bit superior.

Finally we can cast off the vest of personal security, toss away the cap of charm and flair, and retire our umbrella of conspicuous consumption to the recycle bin.

With that last relinquishing, we have been stripped of an old *habit*. Habit is a word used to refer to the distinctive garb of monks and nuns, but it also can mean the things we do regularly day by day. With that old habit gone, we stand naked. It's uncomfortable, but it may help us to realize that those old clothes did not help us touch and be touched. Instead they dressed us up for loneliness, the loneliness of a dog-eat-dog world, a world that pitted us against our "flesh and blood" surroundings.

Our text says quite clearly, however, our battle is *not* against flesh and blood, but against "the rulers, authorities, the powers of this dark world and against the spiritual forces of evil in the heavenly realms." In other words, we battle not only devils and demons but systems of greed, hate, and violence that trap us and oppress the poor and needy. The battle is against voices that tempt you, cultural values that lure you, and false prophets that lie to you.

We do not, however, fight back with the same weapons. We wage peace rather than war, and our equipment for peace-waging is forged in the armory of heaven. We put on the full armor of God. A *new* habit.

First we wrap ourselves in the belt of truth, the truth that centers us and holds our gravity. This is the truth of Jesus, the Christ, who shows us that the power of love is greater than the love of power, that life is stronger than death, that beauty is stronger than ugliness.

Next we don a breastplate forged from one material, the steel of deep integrity. This enables us to live for one Lord and one kingdom, all the time, and no longer live with two sets of rules.

We need the swift shoes of peace that ready our feet for mercy at a moment's notice. Vital too is the shield of faith that protects us from the arrows of despair, doubt, and division. The helmet of God's grace and love, which is our first and last hope, fits snug and true. Finally, our only offensive weapon: the sword of the Spirit, which is God's Word.

This is our beautiful new habit as disciples. The goal is no longer to look out for number one, but rather to follow the leader, Jesus. Dressed in this way, we can courageously march into the day with a prayer for God's wisdom, ready to resist the powers and engage the enemies we are called to love.

Talk It Over

1. Can you think of an additional piece of "clothing" that we often wear in our culture and need to pull off?

2. Can you think of an additional piece of armor that the Bible elsewhere might suggest to us?

3. Can you describe a recent "spiritual battle" that you have been a part of?

In Other Words

"There are two equal and opposite errors into which our race can fall about the devils. One is to disbelieve in their existence. The other is to believe, and to feel an excessive and unhealthy interest in them. They themselves are equally pleased by both errors, and hail a materialist or a magician with the same delight."

—C. S. Lewis, *The Screwtape Letters*

Do Something!

Have a special "dress-up" dinner together as a group. Invite all your guests to bring along some clothes they rarely wear. Collect them in a box and donate them to a local charity.

Weapon 6

"The tempter came . . . to him. . . .
But [Jesus] answered, 'It is written,
"One does not live by bread alone,
but by every word that comes
from the mouth of God."'"

—Matthew 4:3-4, NRSV

"Take . . . the sword of the spirit,
which is the word of God."

—Ephesians 6:17

In September 2006, Hurricane Florence hit the south coast of Newfoundland with tremendous force. Liz Durnford was watching TV in her three-year-old bungalow perched on a rocky escarpment on the edge of the Atlantic Ocean in Francois, a small hamlet of one hundred people, when she felt the house shake.

Here, in her words, is what she did then: "I picked up my Bible to hold the wind back. I'm not religious or anything, but I do believe in God, and something was telling me, 'If you take your Bible, somebody's watching over you.'" After grabbing her Bible she got out of there. Moments later her house was swept toward the ocean.

The picture of this superstitious young woman clutching her Bible as if it were a good-luck charm when everything she owned and

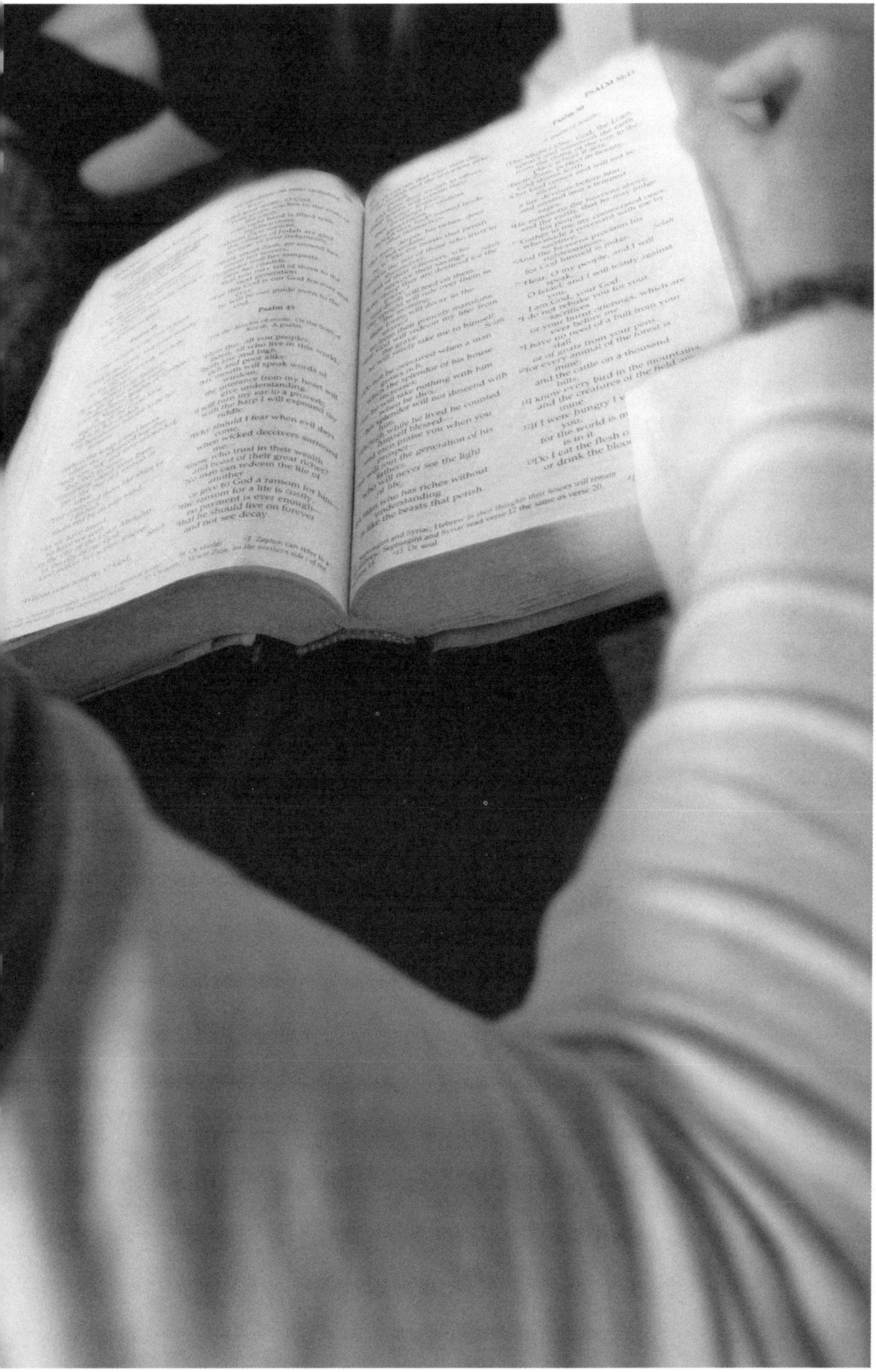
PSALM 50:13
Psalm 49
Psalm 50

her very life was under attack is a striking image. Instinctively, she grabbed on to God's Word like a drowning person grabbing on to a life preserver.

Owning a Bible and opening the Bible, however, are two quite different things. Sadly, many people navigate their way through life in possession of a Bible, which says it is a lamp for our feet, but they rarely turn on its illuminating beam.

Not so the Master! At the beginning of his public ministry, Jesus undertook a forty-day fast that left him terribly hungry and totally depleted. Satan saw his opportunity and moved in, tempting Jesus to rely on himself or on the forces of evil rather than depending on his heavenly Father.

Here's the thing about sustained fasting: it saps your energy and weakens your immune system. The public saw this firsthand in England when it was invited to watch magician David Blaine test his endurance in 2003 by living only on water for the forty-four days that he spent in a Plexiglas cage hanging from a crane near the Tower of London.

Like David Blaine, Jesus probably also exhibited symptoms such as dizziness and loss of strength during his fast. But despite being physically weak and very vulnerable to attack, Jesus was neither helpless nor defenseless. Why? He had "the sword of the spirit, which is the word of God." Three times Jesus said, "It is written," followed by a relevant verse from the book of Deuteronomy. After the third Bible quote, wielded as a weapon, "the devil left him and angels came and attended him" (Matt. 4:11).

Taking his cue, the Master's disciples do not allow the Bible to collect dust on a shelf. Followers of Jesus work at knowing the Bible well enough to be able to say, "It is written," not only to fight temptation but also to encourage and to be encouraged.

For several years I followed a program that allowed me to read through the entire Bible in one year. I was frequently amazed by the serendipitous way that something I would read in God's Word in the morning would arm me for something experienced later that day.

On one occasion, for example, I was on the phone with my brother, a pastor. He told me that he was feeling down because he was preparing to do the funeral of a teenaged girl who had died after a drawn-out battle with cancer. I had just read Isaiah 43 that morning, so I shared the part where God says: "When you pass through the waters, I will be with you; and when you pass through the rivers, they will not sweep over you. When you walk through the fire, you will not be burned; the flames will not set you ablaze."

When I finished reading this passage, there was silence on his end. Finally he responded, "You won't believe this, but that's exactly the passage we read during my last visit before she died. She asked me to preach on it at her funeral." All I could say was, "No way!" and marvel at the way God spoke the same message to us on opposite ends of the country.

Millions of people own a copy of the Bible. True disciples of Jesus open and read their Bibles and know that they are listening to the beautiful voice of the Master when they do.

In Other Words

"The Bible is a high explosive. . . . It has startled the individual soul in ten thousand different places into a new life, a new world, a new belief, a new conception, a new faith."

—British Prime Minister Stanley Baldwin, 1928

Talk It Over

1. What is your practice of Bible reading?

2. Have you ever thought of reading through the Bible in one year?

3. What keeps you from getting into God's Word?

Do Something!

Play "Sword of the Spirit." In this game, everyone has a Bible and one person is designated to call out a specific Bible verse. When players locate the verse, they raise their Bible up in the air with a finger marking the page. The first person to do so, ready to read it, wins a point. Play until someone reaches 10 points and award that person a prize. Have consolation prizes available too.

Bring 7

> *"The first thing Andrew did was to find his brother Simon and tell him, 'We have found the Messiah.' . . . And he brought him to Jesus."*
>
> —John 1:41-42

He proposed; she said yes. He was thrilled; she was ecstatic. Finally, she was alone in the car heading home. The first thing she did then was to call us, her parents, on her cell phone. Then she called her sister and her best friend.

That's the way it is with good news. The first thing you want to do, no, *have* to do, is tell someone, and the person you tell will usually be someone very important in your life, someone you know well.

After spending an entire day with Jesus, "the first thing Andrew did was to find his brother Simon and tell him, 'We have found the Messiah.'" The phrase "the first thing" tells us about Andrew's emotional state. He was incredibly excited about the day that he had just spent with Jesus. He had to share his feelings with another person.

Why was he so excited?

Like every human being, Andrew was searching for a spiritual leader, for that one Person whose every word can be trusted, whose every action inspires and encourages, who has the power to heal the world's ills and to set everything right.

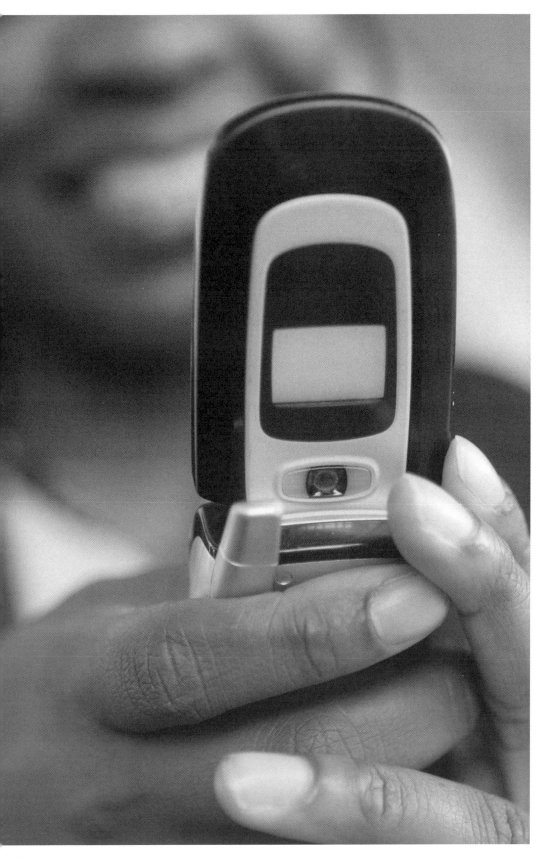

For a while, Andrew thought that John the Baptist might be that person. But John made it abundantly clear that he was merely a minor character making straight the way for the real Messiah. Then Jesus passed by and John said, "Look, the Lamb of God."

That's when Andrew decided to leave John and check out Jesus. What he heard and saw changed his life forever. In the presence of the realization of his deepest longings, his life finally fell into place. He found the Teacher he had been searching for. Life became beautiful. It's no wonder that Andrew just had to find and tell his brother, Simon Peter. Disciples make disciples.

Telling his brother about Jesus, however, is not the *main thing* for which Andrew is remembered. What he is especially remembered for is *"bringing"* his brother to Jesus. Andrew's enthusiasm was so contagious and his invitation was so intentional that Simon Peter could not resist and went with Andrew to meet Jesus himself.

But how do we do what Andrew did? How do we bring to Christ someone who is still searching, who is able to resonate U2's heart-wrenching cry "I still haven't found what I'm looking for!" (*The Joshua Tree*). How do we invite someone who is still lost become a disciple?

Andrew did three simple things: he spent time with Jesus; he shared his excitement with someone close to him; and he invited that person to the place where Jesus was. Andrew asked, "Rabbi, where are you staying?" Jesus replied, "Come and you will see!" Andrew was overwhelmed; Jesus rejoiced. And when Andrew was finally alone again, he headed straight for the person who meant the most to him: his brother.

In our culture we live under the subtle, silencing pressure that faith is a personal hobby or a private matter. In contrast to this, Andrew refused to contain his joy.

That's the way it is with good news!

Talk It Over

1. Do you feel that sharing faith is an invasion of privacy?

2. Who comes to mind as the first person you would love to bring to Jesus?

3. What's stopping you?

In Other Words

When you know a pretty story, you don't let it go unsaid.
You tell it to your children as you tuck them into bed.
When you know a wonderful secret, you tell it to your friends,
tell 'em a lifetime filled with Jesus is like a street that never ends.

—Larry Norman, "Sweet, Sweet Song of Salvation," *Upon This Rock*

Do Something!

Encourage your church to plan an activity or worship service that is specifically geared toward newcomers. Extend an invitation to this event to someone you know who does not attend church or know the Lord.

Earth 8

> *"Be fruitful and increase in number;*
> *fill the earth and subdue it. Rule over the fish*
> *in the sea and the birds in the sky and over*
> *every living creature that moves on the ground."*
> —Genesis 1:28

Can you imagine the jungle that stood before Adam? It's called a garden in Genesis, but it would have had no paths, no gazebos, and I'm sure few of the hedges were trimmed. It was bustling and bursting with the wildness of life.

In the midst of this, God calls Adam to be the manager and caretaker of it all. He is called to domesticate, to develop, to have dominion over this vast and diverse creation. You can imagine Adam, like the first pioneer, gritting his teeth and leaning into the work of clearing a space to sit down and rest.

Discipleship as we have been exploring it is not some other-worldly New Testament invention. Discipleship is a continuation of God's call to all human beings to be God's representative agents on the earth. It is a renewal of that original vocation. While the first disciples were beckoned away from their fishnets, they were recommissioned for the strategic purpose of calling others to make Jesus the Lord of their life—no matter what job they had.

Jesus was ushering in a kingdom, a new earth, and that kingdom was evidenced in people who lived out their occupations according to his commands. Fishermen included.

What does that mean for us in the postmodern world? A recent study published in the journal *Science* estimates that by 2048 the world will have depleted all its seafood as a result of overfishing, pollution, and other environmental factors. Already in 2003 scientists calculated that 29 percent of fish species had collapsed, meaning they were over 90 percent below their historic maximum catch levels. It appears that we have horribly abused our position as God's appointed rulers of creation. A religion of human greed and exploitation has taken over the divine charge to rule well, and this stirs up a deep sense of sorrow in many people.

Some react by saying the problem was caused by the Bible—specifically God's call for humans to "have dominion" as some translations have it. Journalist Matthew Scully's book *Dominion: The Power of Man, the Suffering of Animals, and the Call to Mercy* (St. Martins, 2002) is a passionate plea for human beings to take responsibility for this mess. Scully confesses he is not a particularly devout or pious man, but he agrees with God's call in Genesis. He says the gifts of animals, "the ones their Creator intended for them, are good for many things—governing just isn't one of them." The obligation for creation care must lie with us.

As disciples, we must remind ourselves that our Lord died not just for our souls but for the renewal of all creation. Our stewardship and even partnership with creation is part of that restoration. Saint Francis of Assisi was a disciple who befriended wolves and helped earthworms across roadways. He recognized "Brother Sun" and "Sister Moon" as fellow creatures of God, similarly called to give God glory with all their being.

We may want to be careful around bears, but the idea that we care for the plants and animals of this planet is as old as Adam. We can lobby for restrictions on fishing and for the development of fish farms. We can buy local foods wherever possible and conscientiously compost and recycle our waste. This is our Reformed, Christian confession: discipleship is a beautiful calling as deep as the deepest depths of ocean and as wide as the infinite spaces of the universe itself—because God's redeeming love is that all-encompassing.

Talk It Over

1. One of the authors of this book buys meat from an Old Order Mennonite farmer who cares conscientiously for his cattle. What other examples of good "ruling" or stewardship do you know of?

2. In what ways might you practice better caretaking of the earth?

In Other Words

"Our destruction of nature is not just bad stewardship, or stupid economics, or a betrayal of family responsibility; it is the most horrid blasphemy."

—Wendell Berry, *Sex, Economy, Freedom and Community*

Do Something!

Some people follow what is called a "100-mile diet." This is an attempt to only eat foods grown in a 100-mile radius of one's home in order to support local farmers, avoid excess transportation and pollution costs, and mitigate the exploitation of land and people in developing countries. Plan a meal this week that follows the 100-mile diet.

Interruption 9

"So Abram went, as the Lord had told him. . . ."
—Genesis 12:4

A Christian doctor had a nice family practice in our town. All her kids were in school and life seemed to flow sweet and smooth. Then her work with local AIDS patients blossomed into a calling to start an AIDS clinic in town. The construction of the clinic led to a passion to help stop the spread of the epidemic in Africa. Soon she was challenging multiple cities in Ontario to raise millions of dollars for needy clinics in Africa, and her quiet life of clinic work became a global humanitarian relief campaign.

Discipleship is often, if not always, a matter of divine interruption. Abraham and Sarah, two characters at the beginning of the Old Testament, remind us of that.

Imagine the scene. Abraham and Sarah live comfortably in the land of Ur. They are well settled; no doubt they have plans for a stable working life followed by a quiet retirement in a bungalow along the banks of the Euphrates River. They are saving up their gold and silver to ensure that they don't have to be anxious about maintaining their standard of living as they age.

Then comes the call of God, and the plans God lays out are drastically different from their own. God wants Abraham to leave his home-

town and wander off to some uncertain place. This call is a radical interruption of life, yet it is somehow part of a great project God has for the blessing of all nations. It's God's first gospel call.

Genesis doesn't describe the questions Sarah and Abraham had about this new direction. It doesn't describe the marital tensions that arose as these two ninety-year-olds packed up the camels for the big move. It only says, "So Abraham left." They hit the road.

We see this again in the New Testament as Jesus interrupts the disciples in their fishing, tax collecting, and fig tree meditations to say "Follow me." And boom—off they go.

Old Testament theologian Walter Brueggemann says that God's call is not just a request to sign on to membership in a club. It is "a summons away from our characteristic safety nets of social support" to follow a leader who models a way of life contrary to the old habits of the world around us. When God calls us to discipleship, we give up the "reality" of consumerism, individualism, and competition for success and security and take on a new reality —God's mission to bless all nations.

Disciples have their lives redirected in ways that may seem inopportune, but at the heart of it all is a love for all nations. We are called to live as Jesus did: teaching, preaching, healing—addressing whatever needs grab our holy passion—for the good of the world.

A student who had just converted to the Christian faith stopped by my campus office. "It's like day and night," he said. "Before, I just didn't care about people. Now I do. You should have seen me before. Now I want to serve. I'm on a new road."

Whether recent convert or long-time Christian, we are on a new road and building a new and different reality from the one that

people take for granted in our satellite TV world. God interrupts the world in its power plays and pain, and offers blessing for all nations.

Talk It Over

1. How has God interrupted your life? What new roads has he called you to travel?

2. There is a lot of pressure in mass media today urging even very young people to think about their retirement years. What are you planning for your retirement, and where is the beauty of discipleship in it?

In Other Words

"All the world is a book, and those who do not travel read only a page."

—St. Augustine

Do Something!

Find a local charity that is looking for volunteers or sponsoring a fund-raising campaign. Offer your time, skills, and energy without expectation of reward.

Run 10

"After a while his master's wife took notice of Joseph and said, 'Come to bed with me.' But he refused."

—Genesis 39:7-8

Potiphar's wife was lonely and bored. Her husband was often gone, happily leaving his household in the capable hands of the young, handsome slave he had recently purchased from some foreign traders. She was unhappy, an emotional and spiritual vacuum waiting to be filled.

Joseph was full of tears and testosterone. He was devastated by the shattering experience of being sold into slavery by his own brothers. Far from the restraining influence of his family and his faith community, he had every reason in the world to reject their values and rebel against God. He must have been unsettled— a psychological and physical time bomb ready to explode.

On a given day, opportunity presented itself. Two vulnerable people in daily proximity passed in a hallway. She made her move: "Come to bed with me." The ground was fertile for a steep slide into sin. Somewhere, a demonic chortle could be faintly heard.

Amazingly, considering Joseph's situation and his own sexual needs, he refused. She tried again, day after day. She looked for ways to be near him. She constantly asked him to sleep with

her. Steadfastly he said no. He did everything he could to avoid her until she finally grabbed him in frustration. When he refused again and ran out of the house, she screamed, "Rape!" The rest is redemptive history. God's plan to protect his people through Joseph could not be thwarted.

Through his refusals, Joseph showed himself to be a beautiful disciple, able to say yes to whatever helped his spiritual walk and no to whatever hindered it.

Why did he say no to Potiphar's wife? We know of at least three reasons:

- Joseph had a living relationship with God. The story constantly mentions that the Lord was with him in difficult times. In the pit, in slavery, in prison, and in Pharaoh's court, Joseph was always aware of God's presence.
- Joseph also felt a great sense of responsibility to his human master. He refused to privately betray or jeopardize the trust Potiphar had placed in him. For Joseph, slavery and imprisonment were not reasons to care less, but opportunities to really care.
- Finally, Joseph had a strong sense of calling. The two dreams that had caused his siblings to be so angry with him had convinced him that he was on this planet for a purpose that God would clarify sooner or later.

How did he say no to sexual temptation? He made life simple by simply saying no. He did not waver; he did not waffle. He did not open the door even a crack. He did not send out any vibes that he was available. He just said no.

We also know that he ran. This is a time-honored, biblical strategy. Paul wrote "Flee from sexual immorality" and "flee from idolatry" (1 Cor. 6:18; 10:14). Smart advice! Just run from danger. Smart young man, this Joseph! He knew enough to sprint out of the house.

Even the smartest people in the world have discovered that sin makes you stupid. Joseph avoided the idiocy of an illicit affair with a simple strategy effective enough to keep the dumbest person out of trouble: he refused and he ran.

Disciples of Jesus remember how to walk and know how to run. Keep that in mind the next time you're a flirtatious comment or a point-and-click away from disappointing your Master and hurting someone you love.

Talk It Over

1. Sexual temptations are not the only kind of temptations we face. How else are you tempted?

2. What would refusing and running look like for you?

3. If you are struggling with sexual or any other kind of temptation and don't see a way out, what kind of help can you pursue?

In Other Words

"Sex is like dynamite. If it is used in the right place and at the right time the results can be beneficial, but unless the proper regulations are observed there can only be a disastrous explosion. Those people who indulge in sexual activity as casually as they would down a couple of cocktails are always the sort of people who would find it amusing to play with matches in a bomb factory."

—Susan Howatch, *Ultimate Prizes*

Do Something!

Beginning now, fast from watching TV for the next 24 hours. Monitor what you missed and what you gained from the experience.

Mission 11

*"Now, go. I am sending you to Pharaoh
to bring my people the Israelites out of Egypt."*

—Exodus 3:10

"I am the shyest person you'll ever meet," said one Christian teacher. "In fact, when I enter a room I am always worried I'm taking up too much oxygen for the other people present. It is a great joke that God has called me to a life of public speaking."

God's most beautiful works are often accomplished through the oddest disciples. Commentator Walter Brueggemann notes a comic element in the story of the calling of Moses, and not only because Moses had the same feelings about public speaking.

The story goes like this. God appears to Moses in a burning bush, a spectacular display of mystery and might. Then he says to timid Moses: "I have heard the cry of my people who have been made slaves in Egypt. I know their misery, and I will rescue them from their oppressors and bring them to a land of great abundance."

You would then expect the Lord of the universe to say next, "So I'm going to free the Hebrew people." Instead, his next words are, "So I'm sending *you* to liberate them from their captivity."

What? The mysterious and mighty God of the burning bush is going to send one human being into the totalitarian regime of

the Egyptians to rescue over a million people? How is one man going to subvert the giant political-economic machine of Egyptian power?

This is the remarkable thing about being a disciple: God wants *us* to do his mission. God wants us to be in the places in our world where people are being exploited or treated in unfriendly ways and help them find a way out. This may mean confronting big governments, transnational companies, or other institutional—even religious—powers and advocating, protesting, or prophesying. God calls us to a mission of setting people free.

Jamie VanderBerg, the campus minister at the University of Guelph in Ontario, gathered students who wanted to organize a "Make Poverty History" campaign on their campus. Were they nuts? Undergraduate students standing up against a worldwide system of "haves" and "have nots" with homemade signs and peaceful demonstrations? It's ridiculous, but this is how God works. Liberation doesn't always happen overnight. But it definitely begins when disciples with a mission are on the move.

Thankfully, we don't do it alone. For one thing, God allowed Aaron to stand alongside Moses as a colleague. More important, God himself surrounded Moses. The mission began with God; it was successful through the power of God; and it ended with God's people on the other side of the Red Sea. God sends us, but it is God's mission from beginning to end.

Talk It Over

1. Can you see God's humor in the Scriptures? Can you see it in your own life?

2. What political or economic power would you compare to Egypt?

3. What mission might God be calling you to do?

In Other Words

"Become a revolutionary. Practice your faith."

—Bumper sticker

Do Something!

Register online at the Micah 6:8 Challenge website (www.micahchallenge.org) or the "Make Poverty History" website (www.one.org). Follow that up with a letter to your local government representative expressing concern for alleviating global poverty.

Habitat 12

"I am the LORD your God, who brought you out of Egypt, out of the land of slavery."

—Exodus 20:2

This may be the most important verse for disciples of Christ to remember. It's so important that if you miss it, you've missed what both God and discipleship are all about.

Imagine that a church group decides to build Ethan a house, and they give it to him and his three kids, free and clear. After moving in, something stirs inside Ethan's soul. He becomes anxious. He scrambles around town, finds three jobs, and works himself to the bone, never enjoying a moment's rest. He saves up all the money he earns over the next twenty years. Then one day he stumbles to the church office and lays the money on the desk.

"Here you go," he says to the church secretary. "I've finally paid it all off," he explains, collapsing on the floor in a heap.

The church secretary leans over her desk, over the pile of money, and stares at Ethan. "Uh, you didn't owe us anything," she says. "It was a gift."

It was a gift. This is what every disciple needs to live by every day. Life as God's student is a gift. There is nothing we can do to make it cost more, and there is nothing we can do to make it cost less. It is that beautiful.

You see, the Ten Commandments were given *after* the Israelites were rescued out of Egypt. God reminds them *before* he lays out the rules for living that their freedom is a gift. So the rules are really more like "freedom frameworks"—commandments on how to live as God's rescued people—than they are conditions for receiving God's favor.

The same goes for us. We do not practice discipleship in order to be loved by God and received into his school. God has invited us into his school, and we take on these divine assignments and projects because we are grateful for our admission.

Now imagine that Ethan accepts the house. But he never mows the lawn or repairs the roof shingles when they wear out. He never vacuums the carpet or wipes the counters. He shuns guests. Eventually all this neglect ends when the flame of a candle used in an attempt to spice up the foul air ignites a nearby curtain and causes a devastating fire.

Church members come by the next day, shaking their heads.

"It was a gift, anyway, right?" says Ethan, standing before the ashes.

Ethan may be technically right, but he has missed out on the full experience of the gift. This is like the Israelites who, given full freedom to worship and grow without persecution, then construct an idol of metal and bow down to it. Their freedom from Egypt is not fully what it could have been. They did not steward their rescue well.

Now imagine that Israel had seized their freedom for the greatest good. That would be like Ethan and his kids celebrating their new house with abandon. They plant a vegetable garden in the yard, invite friends over for corn roasts, buy art from the local Salvation Army thrift store to grace the living room walls. They save some money on the side. Over time, they donate back to the church so others can be given homes as well.

One neighbor asks over the fence: "Hey—why do you guys work so hard on your house?"

"Because it's a gift," Ethan replies with a smile.

Discipleship is an act of love in response to an act of love, which summarizes what the commandments are at their heart. Love for God and the stranger next door. Something to make the heart swell with thanks!

Talk It Over

1. How much of our discipleship is an attempt to earn God's kindness?

2. Pastor Dietrich Bonhoeffer was martyred for his resistance to the Nazis during World War II. In *The Cost of Discipleship* he compared "cheap grace"—forgiveness without repentance and communion without confession, with "costly grace"—a divine sacrifice of love that impels us to obedient discipleship. How do we at times take grace for granted? In what ways does our discipleship come with a cost to us?

3. How do you treat the gifts you have been given over the years?

In Other Words

"I do not at all understand the mystery of grace—only that it meets us where we are, but does not leave us where it found us."

—Anne Lamott, *Traveling Mercies*

Do Something!

Think of someone you know who could use some help cleaning house, mowing the lawn, or shoveling snow. Then do it at least once for free.

Magnet 13

"One thing I ask from the LORD, this only do I seek: that I may dwell in the house of the LORD all the days of my life, to gaze upon the beauty of the LORD."

—Psalm 27:4

Jesus' profile probably didn't have the chiseled features that the advertising industry prizes. He may not have had the sculpted body of a personal trainer. His teeth were likely not pearly white. It's doubtful he had the smooth and unblemished skin portrayed in Warner Sallman's famous *Head of Christ*. In short, Jesus' attraction wasn't based on the standards of beauty that are the sexual ideal according to Hollywood and the fashion industry. He turned heads, but not the way an attractive man or woman entering a restaurant does.

Interestingly, not one of Jesus' peers left us a physical description of him. Our picture of him has been entirely influenced by the imagination of artists. Somehow, we have formed such a clear, collective image of Jesus as a brown-eyed, blond-haired, bearded hippie that we know exactly what we mean when someone says, "He looks just like Jesus." And we would only say this about someone who looks like James Caviezel playing Jesus in *The Passion of the Christ*.

The prophet Isaiah, on the other hand, gave us a rough description of what the Messiah would look like seven hundred years before

Jesus was born. Inspired by the Holy Spirit, Isaiah wrote, "He had no beauty or majesty to attract us to him, nothing in his appearance that we should desire him." In fact, he turned heads away "like one from whom people hide their faces" (Isa. 53:2-3). Jesus was not a beautiful man. But he lived a beautiful life.

Jesus' gentle, loving presence magnetically attracted people to him. Those who were shunned by others found acceptance from him. Mothers approached him, lepers ran to him, and children climbed onto his lap. Men and women who spent time with Jesus experienced love that is patient and kind; love that is not self-seeking or easily angered; love that always protects, hopes, trusts, and perseveres.

Jesus practiced the principles of the peaceful kingdom of God. He treated women with ultimate respect. He embraced bruised spirits with the gentlest arms. He held the last and the lost in the highest regard. He healed the sick, comforted the mourners, gave hope to the prisoners, and fed the hungry. He showed an upside-down world what life right side up really is.

Jesus enjoyed life with his Father in Heaven. Every searching son and every wandering daughter was shown the way home to a divine parent who not only knew enough to let go but also cared enough to welcome him or her back home.

Jesus turned an ugly death into an expression of such sacrificial love that a crude cross has become a universal symbol of love at its best. Not content only to turn his brutal death into an opportunity to forgive his enemies, he also transformed the messy stories of guilty sinners into delightful poems of surprised saints.

In Philippians 4, the apostle Paul invites us to think about whatever is pure and lovely. There is nothing purer or lovelier to think about than the beautiful life that Jesus lived. So gaze upon the beauty of the Lord.

Talk It Over

1. How have you been picturing Jesus? What do you think a Palestinian Jew really looks like?

2. What do you find most beautiful about Jesus?

In Other Words

"Beauty will save the world."

—Fyodor Dostoevsky, *The Idiot*

Do Something!

Draw a picture of what you think Jesus actually looked like. Be sure to color it.

Frog 14

*"Your beauty should not come from outward
adornment, such as elaborate hairstyles
and the wearing of gold jewelry and fine clothes.
Rather, it should be that of your inner self,
the unfading beauty of a gentle and quiet spirit,
which is of great worth in God's sight."*

—1 Peter 3:3-4

We live in a culture so obsessed with outward beauty that for some men and women of a certain age, surgical procedures promising to make us look better are as popular a commodity as bottled water and bagged ice during a power shortage. Even teens, still developing, fantasize about medical procedures to help them lose inches here and add inches there in a futile quest to measure up to fashion and Hollywood-inspired ideals that few can attain.

Into this madness, the apostle Peter's words bring some needed sanity. If he were writing today, he might say, "Your beauty should not come from silicone implants, Botox injections, laser treatments, hair dyes, or designer clothing and accessories. Instead, it should be that of your inner self, the unfading beauty of a gentle and quiet spirit, which is of great worth in God's sight."

In all the ways that really matter, Jesus is the most beautiful person who ever walked on earth. The invitation to be his disciple

is nothing more and nothing less than an invitation to the same beautiful life that he lived. It's an invitation to take up our cross and follow him. And become beautiful in the eye of the Beholder.

The life of a disciple is usually pictured as a life of struggle and denial. And it is that. It is also characterized as a life of do's and don'ts that turns its back on the easy way and looks for God's help to choose the hard way. It is that as well. Dietrich Bonhoeffer's *The Cost of Discipleship*, which deals with the suffering that discipleship entails, is a powerful reminder that following Jesus puts you on the Via Dolorosa too. The way of suffering is a difficult road and Christians are not exempt from the hatred and persecution that Jesus faced. The Lord made that crystal clear.

At the same time, however, we should not forget that a Christ-centered, spirit-led life is a beautiful life. The "unfading beauty of a gentle and quiet spirit" that Peter talks about is such an attractive quality. The fruit of the Spirit—love, joy, peace, patience, kindness, goodness, faithfulness, gentleness, and self-control—shine with incandescent brilliance. The teachings of the Sermon on the Mount that Jesus preached and practiced are magnetic when lived out in a person's life. And they add up to a beauty that is much more than skin-deep, a beauty that is heart-deep.

Stories like *Beauty and the Beast* and *The Frog Prince* remind us that when we look beyond an imperfect outward appearance, we may recognize the kind of inward, unfading beauty that the apostle Peter had in mind. These stories remind us that humans "look at the outward appearance, but the LORD looks at the heart" (1 Sam. 16:7).

Our society's obsession with outward appearance focuses on superficial, arbitrary standards of beauty. Discipleship, on the other hand,

recognizes that the frog is already a beautiful person long before the story ends with his transformation into a handsome prince.

So let's celebrate the beautiful life Jesus offers. The call to discipleship is a call to follow our beautiful Savior, and to become a beautiful person too. Beautiful in the ways that really matter.

Talk It Over

1. In what ways do you feel our culture's pressure to put image before substance?

2. What are you going to do about it?

3. What might be some good reasons to be attentive to your appearance?

4. Where do you draw the line? Why?

In Other Words

"People are like stained glass windows: they sparkle and shine when the sun is out, but when the darkness sets in, their true beauty is revealed only if there is light within."

—Elisabeth Kübler-Ross

Do Something!

Read a book or view a movie based on one of the fables mentioned in this devotional reading. Share the experience with members of your family or small group.

Nonsense 15

*"When he came to his senses, he said,
'How many of my father's hired men have food
to spare, and here I am starving to death!'"*
—Luke 15:17

Sociologist Georg Simmel argued that life in the city is overstimulating —the noisy traffic, jackhammers, bustling crowds, and relentless media advertising. People react by insulating themselves with a protective psychological shell. This shell that protects becomes the shell that desensitizes us.

This is a significant observation because God often works powerfully through our feelings. In the story of the wandering son, feelings are the critical point—the turning point—in the story. Verse 17 describes it as the point "when he came to his senses."

Think about it: "when he came to his senses." This kind of language tells us that he had not been in touch with his senses for quite some time. Maybe he was living the life of a reactionary, so determined *not* to be like his brother or father that he ignored all the other facts and feelings. He pushed on, driven by this unspoken vow to the "wild living" that Luke describes. He bombarded himself with dramatic experiences—new friends, heavy drinking, sexual promiscuity, mind-bending drugs. It was a sensory overload that left his soul numb.

Yet the reactionary son "comes to his senses." Maybe he was shocked to his senses: the putrid smell of the manure squishing

between his toes or the relentless gnawing inside his half-empty stomach suddenly gripped his attention. Or perhaps one day, while a pig nuzzled up to him as he sat in the mud, the thought hit him like a bolt of lightening: This is nonsense! What am I doing here?

You see, God gifted us with all kinds of antennae: we can feel the wing of a bee on our cheek and smell a single drop of perfume in a three-room apartment. We can see a candle flame on a distant hill. At the same time, we can so easily ignore the pain that calls us to turn around and come home. We are too clever for our own good. We fool ourselves.

A woman with an alcohol addiction came to a health care clinic completely burned out. Her self-anesthetizing behavior had led to the loss of her job, and she was estranged from her entire family. But it was as if she had suddenly woken up. She sensed something —call it sorrow—that prompted her to seek help. She is now in recovery with the aid of Alcoholics Anonymous.

Although most translations use the phrase "when he came to his senses" for our text, the actual Greek is more blunt: "when he came to himself." It was as if he had been far from himself—as far from himself as he was far from home. He'd been away in some sort of dream state. Now he was waking up, beginning to see himself as he really was: not a fun-loving playboy but a lonely, hurting, hopeful son.

And then the son turns his life around. This is the raw but beautiful stuff of discipleship. The Bible in other places calls this *repentance*. It involves changing the course of your life, making a fresh start, going back to the One who loves you.

Feelings, especially pain and grief, indicate our need for God. But this moment of conversion, the moment of being moved by God's Spirit, isn't something that happens just once. It happens every time you leave yourself, leave your God-given senses and follow some seductive sensual overload that leaves you numb and cold.

Too often we expect God's presence to be something *sensational*, something that happens once in your life if you're lucky. We expect some overwhelming experience that leaves no space for the un-certainties of daily faith. But conversion is a daily miracle. It may begin in a place as mundane as a pigsty, and it continues all the way home and beyond.

Talk It Over

1. In his book *The Saturated Self* Kenneth J. Gergen suggests that our society suffers from a basic nervousness and anxiety he calls "multiphrenia," caused by a connection to too many different media. Is that your experience too?

2. John Calvin said we come to know God through our misery. Can you think of a time in your life when you "came to your senses" or "came to yourself" out of misery?

3. Is your story of discipleship with Christ dramatic like Paul's or more gradual like Timothy's?

In Other Words

"Gimme what I don't get.
Gimme what you got.
Too much is not enough.
Don't spy I feel numb."
—U2, "Numb," *Zooropa*

"You give me something I can feel."
—U2, "Vertigo," *How to Dismantle an Atomic Bomb*

Do Something!

Put a blindfold on one of the people in your group. Place five different foods or spices on the table in front of her and have her try to guess the identity of each, using all her senses except sight.

Dora 16

"They devoted themselves . . . to fellowship."

—Acts 2:42

An elderly woman in her nineties was totally deaf, but she insisted on always going to church. When asked why, she replied: "I just want people to know which side I'm on."

Dora Benson, a feisty friend of ours, was just like that. She faithfully attended her little church all her life, including the last five years when she became so deaf that she could hardly understand a single word.

Her severe hearing loss prompted family and friends to share some humorous anecdotes at her funeral. Her son-in-law, for example, recalled the time that Dora visited him and asked where her daughter was. "Peggy went to the store to get some cheese," he said. Indignantly, she responded, "What do you mean I have to say please!" After he clarified in writing what he had actually said, she burst out with her beautiful, sunny laugh.

Advanced age and deafness never stopped her from blessing others at church. She smiled at everyone who came, often beckoning people over for a welcoming hug. Often she offered the closing prayer. As all the worshipers stood in a circle for the benediction, someone would speak directly and slowly into her ear and ask, "Will you pray?" Dora would repeat, "Pray?" and then launch into a beautiful, heartfelt prayer addressed straight to Jesus.

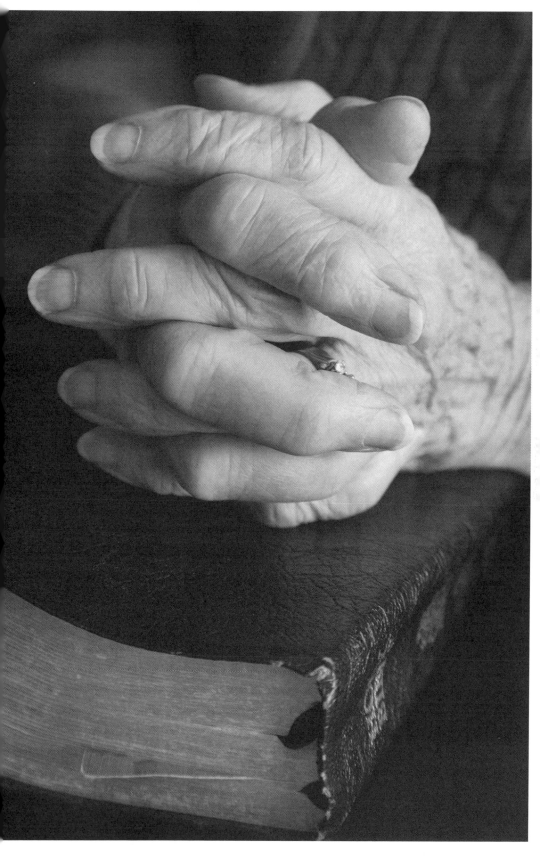

What explained Dora's faithful church attendance until the day she died? She knew that discipleship meant commitment to Christ's community.

But what prompted her commitment in the first place?

She wasn't always a strong spiritual leader and committed Christian. In fact, for the first half of her life she was an alcoholic who often left her nine children alone in order to visit the bars. Sunday mornings were for sending her children to Sunday school and staying home herself to deal with a hangover.

One wintry night, however, she walked past twelve-year-old Evelyn's bedroom and heard her praying, "Dear Lord, please help my mom stop drinking." Her daughter's prayer broke her heart. She vowed then and there to stop drinking and start going to church. She took the very next opportunity to go, and she gave her life to Christ. She was forty-one years old when Jesus rescued her. The next fifty years of faithfulness to her biological family and her church family were her way of thanking her Savior.

Her commitment was severely tested when her son Steward was killed by a car as he crossed the street in front of her house. Disconsolate, she was seriously tempted to turn to the bottle again for comfort. But another daughter went to her and said one of the wisest things that anyone could ever say in such a painful situation. "Mom," she said, "What is faith for if not for something like this?" That was all it took for Dora to cling to her Lord again and to continue coming to church. By faithfully attending, she did more than show whose side she was on; she encouraged others to keep following Jesus too.

In the early church described in Acts we see the same "devotion to fellowship" among the believers who "came together continually" in Jerusalem. Like Dora, they understood what the writer of Hebrews meant when he reminded Jesus' followers to keep meeting together because that's the way Christians "encourage one another."

While Dora got sober and never looked back, many others experience a lifetime of stumbling and turning back to God. The encouragement of the community is often the key to overcoming those setbacks. Part of community is remembering that we don't always get it right the first time.

In the New Testament church and in Dora's life, this is the pattern we see: gratitude for Christ's salvation; commitment to Christ's community; and mutual encouragement for Christ's followers.

Psychologist and author James Kok wrote a book entitled *90% of Helping Is Just Showing Up.* We might paraphrase that title like this: "90 percent of encouraging is just coming together."

Dora was a devoted disciple who understood that. It's important that we understand it too, so that we can bless our church families the way she blessed hers.

Talk It Over

1. What is your practice of church attendance? How significant is it to your spiritual life?

2. How has your commitment to your faith community been tested?

In Other Words

"I wouldn't put up with all this crud if I wasn't called!"

—Jim Schlottman's pastor friend Bruce, *Quiet Waters Compass On-Line*, October 2006

Do Something!

Is any member of your family or small group wearing a ring representing some kind of promise, vow, or special relationship? Pass the ring around as its owner tells the story of how he or she got it.

Lonely 17

> *"My God, my God, why have you abandoned me?"*
>
> —**Matthew 27:46**, *The Message*

One quick way to scatter an audience is to begin to talk about your loneliness. Nothing turns people away faster than giving testimony to the shadowy world of your frustrated attempts at love and friendship. Oddly enough, however, loneliness is a universal feeling that hits even those tightly woven into the fabric of family and faith community. Loneliness is a hurt that can pour into our hearts in unexpected ways.

I wrestled with a singleness I did not desire well into my thirties. I would scurry around at work all day, temporarily distracted from my sadness, but as the sun began its daily descent, I would walk home to a quiet, empty house. Sometimes the absence of others is louder than their presence. The world can seem small and at times even cruel when there is no one to share the tasks of daily life. You learn to become your own best friend.

The Bible is full of lonely people. God saw that Adam was lonely, and so he gifted him with Eve. Elijah, exhausted from spiritual contests and fleeing persecution, moaned from a dark cave on Mount Horeb that he was the only faithful prophet left in the land. Even Jesus himself felt forsaken as his disciples abandoned him near the end and then, as our text says, he cried out that his Father abandoned him on the cross.

Like me, some people try to distract themselves from this ache by pouring themselves into their work. Others turn to various forms of cheap entertainment like Internet pornography or try to self-medicate through alcohol or other drugs. Still others turn on automatic pilot and simply go through the motions day after day. But as disciples of Christ we ought not to run away from this experience. Instead, we can move through it.

Dutch Christian writer Henri Nouwen shows us one way to do this. As a celibate priest, he struggled with loneliness quite often. His suggestion to his readers, however, was to find a way to turn their loneliness into solitude. Solitude, for Nouwen, was not the pursuit of privacy or vacations, but a "furnace of transformation" in which God changes us into more of what he is. In solitude, we come to a heightened awareness of both our vulnerability and God's presence. Solitude can become a place of prayer, and in our prayers we come to more deeply realize that God is with us in our loneliness, and we are God's dearly beloved children.

Knowing this, as disciples of Christ, we are led to reach out to others in their pain and loneliness. We seek to nurture a community of wounded healers, and in our giving and serving to find a way to talk about our hurt. Sharing in this beautiful way is not a narcissistic preoccupation. It is a way of acknowledging the brokenness of all our lives, moving through it, and celebrating the friendship we have with God in Christ. All of our fellowship, service, and worship is an anticipation of the time promised us in Revelation 21-22 where we will celebrate our final communion with God and the saints in the new earth, where there shall be no more mourning or crying or pain.

Talk It Over

1. Do you know any lonely people? How could you be a positive presence for them?

2. Can you think of a time when you felt lonely? How did you respond to it?

3. Jesus had an inner circle of three disciples who were close to him, and then the ring of twelve, plus about seventy-two others who were connected to him in a meaningful way. Do we all have or need such concentric circles of friendship? If so, how can we nurture them?

In Other Words

All the lonely people, where do they all come from?
All the lonely people, where do they all belong?

—John Lennon and Paul McCartney, "Eleanor Rigby"

Do Something!

As a group or alone, create a care package and/or handmade card for someone you know who lives alone or whom you think may be lonely.

Xbox 18

> *"Woe to you, teachers of the law*
> *and Pharisees, you hypocrites! You clean*
> *the outside of the cup and dish, but inside*
> *they are full of greed and self-indulgence."*
> —Matthew 23:25

In Toronto, 2005 was hailed by the media as the Year of the Gun. In a twelve-month period there were seventy-eight homicides, fifty-two of them gun-related. The city reeled as members of youth gangs shot each other in a cycle of revenge that had no end. Finally, when an eighteen-year old was shot and killed while attending the funeral of another slain teen, the *Toronto Star* plastered the words "guns, guns, guns" all over the front page around one huge word: "ENOUGH!"

In my home and on my TV, news coverage about the latest tragic shooting at this funeral was immediately followed by a feature on Microsoft's newest game. I watched incredulously as one of the television hosts played a game on Microsoft's new Xbox 360 in which he stalked and killed others with a gun. "Cool," he said repeatedly, as he kept shooting virtual people to death in realistic detail. This segment was immediately followed by a story about church leaders pleading for a meeting with politicians about gun violence. I could not stop myself from saying "Duh!"

This inconsistency is just one of the many ways that humans are incredibly double-minded. For example, people who are genuinely upset by the increase of violence even in peaceful places like Nickel Mines, Pennsylvania, where eleven girls were shot in an Amish schoolhouse, nevertheless continue to see violent movies like *Kill Bill* and slasher films like *Texas Chainsaw Massacre* and its gory sequels. In another example of inconsistency, people who are honestly concerned about the environment nevertheless prefer using their own cars to public transit, cycling, or walking. Still another example is the hypocrisy of people who are enraged by pedophiles but who somehow fail to see the mainstreaming of porn and its exploitation of children for their own sexual stimulation as a problem.

Society is quick to accuse Christians of hypocrisy. But the truth is that inconsistency in its many forms is evident everywhere, both in and outside the church. A person whose walk exactly matches his or her talk is a rarity.

The call to discipleship is the call to a more consistent life, a more single-minded life. The call to discipleship is an invitation to identify the hypocrisy in our lives and to conform our actions to our words. The call to a beautiful life is the challenge to be that rare person of integrity who, as John Maxwell has said, "welds what we say, think, and do into a whole person so that permission is never granted for one of these to be out of sync."

Integrity. What a wonderful characteristic! It has been identified as one of the most important virtues of leadership. It is defined as a godly life that truly and consistently reflects everything that Jesus taught and lived. It includes honesty, reliability, and purity. A man or woman of integrity is a person after God's own heart (1 Sam. 13:14), a person in whom there is "no guile," to use an older translation of John 1:47.

How do we become such men and women?

It begins with recognizing and admitting the gaps in our own lives between God's will and our walk. It continues with genuine sorrow and a broken heart for our own hypocrisies. It involves constant prayer for the Holy Spirit's refining work in us. It relies fully on the perfect work of the Master to heal us, save us, and forgive us for all the inconsistencies in our lives.

Two news stories lamenting the use of guns bracketing a feature touting a wicked game that turns players into cold, calculating killers obviously makes no sense at all. What is not so obvious is the inherent nonsense of simultaneously trying to follow Jesus and satisfying our baser and selfish instincts. Both are examples of a lack of integrity. Now that we've named it, let's ask the Holy Spirit to help us stop our double-tracking, two-timing ways and to be singularly devoted to the Master in all we say and do.

Talk It Over

1. Why is the world so quick to accuse Christians of hypocrisy?

2. Where do you find inconsistency in your own life?

3. What do you need to do to guard or restore your integrity?

In Other Words

"Image is what people think we are: integrity is what we really are."

—John Maxwell

Do Something!

Today's challenge is to purge your home of something that would sadden Jesus if he were to make a surprise visit. (Surprise! He is visiting already!)

Have each person find one item—a CD, a video game or movie, a magazine or book—that needs to go. Have fun smashing it to smithereens or ripping it up.

Clock 19

"Then he said to them, 'The Sabbath was made for people, not people for the Sabbath.'"

—Mark 2:27

Do you ever wonder how technological advances have changed human society since the ancient times? Do we, as modern disciples, live more complex and perhaps more confined lives?

Consider this deep thought: despite what you might think about computers, it has been said that the printing press was "the invention of the millennium." Mass-produced books have changed human life, not to mention Christianity, in colossal ways. But there is yet a more subtle and pervasive technology that may be even more influential in our lives.

Twentieth-century social scientist Lewis Mumford claimed that "the clock . . . is the key machine of the modern industrial age . . . no other machine is so ubiquitous." The fact that we wouldn't have thought of the clock may only prove the point further. We take it so much for granted that we hardly recognize it as an "invention."

But it is. Rarely do we measure life by natural events like the thaw, or by the phases of the moon, or growing seasons like the harvest. Time has become for us a succession of mathematically isolated instants rather than the organic flow of life in its less predictable but nevertheless regular rhythms. Our lives are so ruled by the clock that we no longer eat when we are hungry, but rather when

it is "lunch hour." We don't go to bed when we are tired but program our bodies so we are tired when it's "bed time."

Leap year is a reminder that our invented system of time does not quite fit reality. Our lives, with our datebooks, alarms, and electronic scheduling, are based on a fiction, the fiction of calculated time measurement. And to the extent that these mathematically sequenced and labeled days, hours, and minutes rule our life without compromise, they have become an idol to which we are the slave, the enclosed matrix in which we live without recognizing that life could be otherwise.

The text from Mark comes in the midst of a story in which some Pharisees were badgering a man because Jesus healed him on the seventh day of the week. This broke the rules. It was out of sequence, and the sequence, they insisted, could not be subverted or overridden. The Sabbath, a day of rest and grace, had become an idol—a tradition that could not be questioned.

One way of knowing an idol is that if it were transgressed or altered or even removed, your whole life and faith would fall apart. Mumford suggests that if our clocks were taken away, one can only "forsee the speedy disruption and eventual collapse of our entire society. The modern industrial regime could do without coal and iron and steam easier than it could do without the clock." In modern terms, think of the Y2K panic. If the clocks in our computers didn't turn over in proper sequence, some said the globe would implode in chaos.

Technologies change the way we live and relate in a multitude of ways. It's important for disciples of Christ to develop an awareness of the ways we depend on them and fear living without them.

Here's an experiment to try: see if you can live without your watch for an entire day. Or maybe even try to avoid using gadgets or machines for a week. Get up when the sun rises and eat when it feels like time to eat. Live by your senses and engage in deeper and more frequent prayer. This is the way people lived for millennia

—including during the time of the Bible. Most people around the globe still live that way today. Maybe this experiment would help us think about the beauty we miss and empathize with the hardships of these brothers and sisters.

Certainly clocks and watches help us regulate our activities in many ways. But disciples are always wary of idols—anything that may replace God as the center of our lives, the One we truly depend on. We need to think about the fictions that seem nonnegotiable in our life and subvert them for God's kingdom of truth and grace.

Talk It Over

1. What other idols does our society depend on?

2. What idols have a hold on your life, and how will you loosen their grip?

3. How do you keep the Sabbath as a gift?

In Other Words

"God walks 'slowly,' because he is love. . . . Love has its speed. It is an inner speed. It is a spiritual speed. It is a different kind of speed from the technological speed to which we are accustomed. . . . It goes on in the depth of our life, whether we notice or not, whether we are currently hit by storm or not, at three miles an hour. It is the speed we walk and therefore the speed the love of God walks."

—Kosuke Koyam, *Three Mile-an-Hour God*

Do Something!

Except for work or emergencies, put your cell phone (and other phones) into cold storage for two days. Make every effort to talk to people only face-to-face.

Newsstand 20

"Come to me, all you who are weary and burdened, and I will give you rest. Take my yoke upon you and learn from me, for I am gentle and humble in heart, and you will find rest for your souls. For my yoke is easy and my burden is light."

—Matthew 11:28-30

Deep down, everyone longs for a simpler life. Deeper down, all of us know that we are our own worst enemies in achieving that kind of life.

Simon Whitfield, the triathlete who won gold for Canada at the 2000 Olympics in Australia, did something about that longing for simplicity. After his Olympic success he moved to an artistic and ecologically sensitive community in Saltspring Island, British Columbia. By adopting a simpler lifestyle, he feels less driven and generally happier. Whereas he used to be the kind of person who had to have the latest gadget, he says that he is now more easily content with what he already has.

Like Whitfield, many city folks also dream of a more restful life. As part of that dream, they may buy a cottage or cabin, imagining idyllic days, an easy-going lifestyle, and less stress. Unfortunately, many of them end up applying urban standards to their new rural surroundings. The result? Cottages that are more accurately called houses, lawns that take hours to tend, and double mortgages that

force people to work even harder to make the payments. Is this the simple life? More like the frantic life.

So what's the answer? Changing our exterior surroundings can help to some degree. A restful room in our homes or a favorite place to retreat can do wonders for our harassed spirits. But nothing works like changing our interior landscape. That's where Jesus comes in.

"Come to me, all you who are weary and burdened," Jesus said. "I will give you rest."

Before he says, "Go," to disciples Jesus says, "Come." I visualize him patting the space beside him, inviting me to come and sit for a spell. I imagine him speaking directly to my heart with words that confront me and also comfort me. As I visualize myself sitting beside him and taking in his wonderful words, I can feel my spirit lifting, my courage returning, and my sense of purpose sharpening. By relinquishing control and allowing Jesus to be my Master, I receive his beautiful gift of shalom.

Most of our cultural role models are restless people who have become celebrities by virtue of their relentless pursuit of fame, wealth, or success. "Do this," one person says. "No, that," advises someone else. The next time you look at a newsstand stocked with magazines, remember that the pictures on most of the covers feature the current crop of driven celebrities pushing our world to the brink of insanity.

Tragically, contemporary Christianity is often more a reflection of our driven culture than a countercultural model of a different way of life, a truly restful life. By focusing on programs instead of relationships, the church is often guilty of leaving people lonely for the personal touch that everyone needs. By emphasizing legalities and impossible standards of holiness and purity, church leaders often place unbearable yokes on weary shoulders.

Jesus does not do any of that. "I am gentle and humble in heart," he says, showing us his interior landscape. "My yoke is easy and my burden is light," he concludes, offering us a simpler life built on the gentle peace that he lived to give.

The call to discipleship is a call to a simpler life, a gentler life, a more contented life. It is about letting Jesus quietly sit in your heart. It gains control by giving control over to the Master. It finds rest by losing anxiety through the restful realization that the Lord is near.

Talk It Over

1. Where do you feel harassed or driven?

2. How can you restore simplicity to your life? Where will you begin?

3. Is it possible to be restful while working hard?

In Other Words

"Strong cultural pressures at Christmas and throughout the year lead many to live and celebrate in ways that are neither fulfilling or joyful. Voluntary simplicity says we will find happiness and meaning in life through relationships—within ourselves, with others, with the earth, and with God."

—Gerald Iversen, *Alternatives for Simple Living*

Do Something!

Clip pictures of celebrities (business, sports, Hollywood) and make a collage from magazine covers and newspapers that come into your home. As you cut and paste, discuss why our culture values them and how that compares with biblical ideals.

Fire 21

> *"Do not be afraid. I bring you good news
> of great joy that will be for all the people."*
> —Luke 2:10

A girl and her father were visiting a farm one day. The daughter looked intently at the horse in the barn. "He's all ready to go to church," she said.

The father was confused. "What do you mean?"

"Well, he's already got a long face," she replied.

Some Christians give the joy of the Lord a pretty sour face. John Calvin, for example, has never been known for his giddy sense of humor. In fact, he suffered from tremendous bouts of anxiety. Evaluating his *Institutes of the Christian Religion*, someone has commented, perhaps unfairly, that it has "a petulant and irritable tone, occasionally verging on the cantankerous." Does that sound like some people you know? How about yourself?

The angels that appeared to the shepherds promised good news of *great joy*: God with us in the form of a baby. That same baby echoes the angels by saying to his disciples much later: "I came that my joy may be in you and your joy may be complete." What has happened to that joy?

Sometimes we grow up too quickly. We become serious, if not cynical, and call it the weight of experience. The joy was beaten

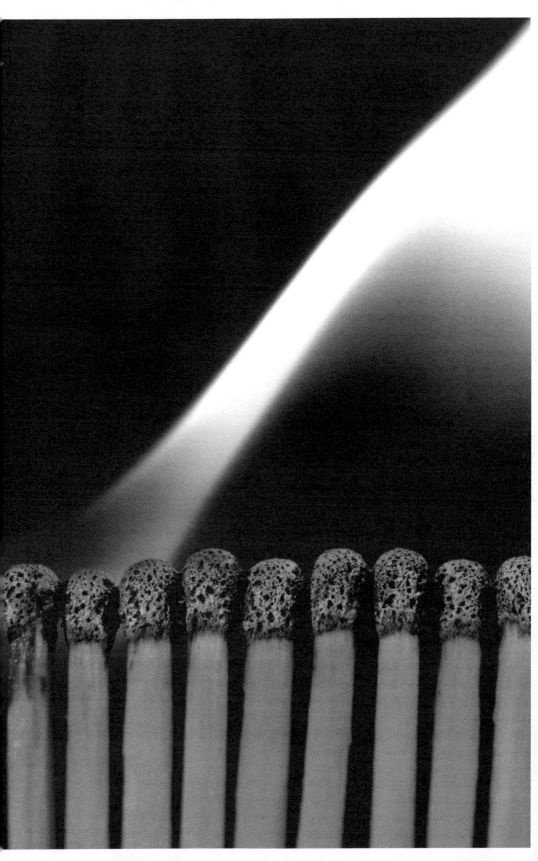

out of us by time and neglect, and we sing "Joy to the World" with bowed heads. It's not that we have lost faith, but somehow, our cup of joy is half-full. Or half-empty.

How do we grow in joy? One day the disciples wanted to remove the children from around Jesus so the serious spiritual stuff could begin. Jesus told them to wait a minute. He embraced the kids and said that the disciples must become like little children to enter the kingdom of God. Become like kids: what does that mean?

There is no secret recipe. Joy comes mysteriously, most often when you don't make it an object of pursuit. It creeps up on you when you put your questions aside and live fully by receiving and trusting God in Jesus by the Holy Spirit. Receiving and loving infants does that to you, and Jesus Christ is the supreme child, our greatest expectation. Infants proclaim that miracles are the stuff of the universe; new life is as real as their babbles and coos. In the presence of such newness, we are surprised by joy.

A student majoring in math ran into my office on campus one day and exclaimed: "Calvin saved me!" What he meant was that by reading Calvin's *Institutes* in between math classes, he had come to a deeper understanding of the grace of God. He recognized that God's favor did not rest on his good behavior or even on his cheerfulness, but that God's grace always comes first. He only needed to receive it with open arms. This discovery was a cause for great joy. (Remember that the words "joy" and "enjoy" occur countless times in Calvin's writings as consequences of living in God's grace.)

Blaise Pascal was another mathematician, the powerful mind behind the invention of calculus. Grace came to him without any additions, however. Upon his conversion, he wrote in his diary: "I met him . . . not the God of the scientists, but the God of Abraham, Moses and Jacob. Joy, joy, joy! Fire, fire fire! Joy, fire. Joy, fire. Joy, fire. Unspeakable joy, oh, the ecstasy of the joy of the Lord!"

Pascal, mature in mind and serious about math, came to receive Jesus like a little child. John Calvin, sophisticated theologian and preacher, demonstrated in his emphasis on God's sovereign grace that he knew in his frail person that his comfort in life and in death rested in Christ alone. We all come with empty hands to God.

The Westminster Catechism, an expression of faith based on the writings of Calvin, begins with this question and answer: "What is the chief purpose of humanity? To glorify and enjoy God forever." That is simple but true. And in it lies the beautiful heart of discipleship.

Talk It Over

1. In what ways can playfulness be an indication of the presence of God's Spirit?

2. Joy is not the same as perpetual giddiness. How would you distinguish lasting joy from constant happiness?

3. What sorts of things rob you of your joy?

In Other Words

"Pride cannot rise to levity or levitation. Pride is the downward drag of all things into an easy solemnity. . . . Seriousness is not a virtue. . . . For solemnity flows out of men naturally; but laughter is a leap. It is easy to be heavy: hard to be light. Satan fell by the force of gravity."

—G. K. Chesterton, *Orthodoxy*

Do Something!

Share a joke or funny story around the group. If pickings are slim, find a joke book, check the joke page in your denominational magazine, or visit your local library for a wider selection.

Ladder 22

*"Half of the wood he burns in the fire;
over it he prepares his meal. . . . From the rest
he makes a god, his idol; he bows down to it
and worships. He prays to it and says,
'Save me! you are my god!'"*

—Isaiah 44:16-17

Douglas Coupland is a Generation X writer who can't stop telling stories of young people who are lost, bored, wounded, and searching for meaning in their life. In his book *Girlfriend in a Coma*, the end of the world comes to a group of friends. This apocalypse forces them to look back on their lives, realizing that they literally amused themselves to death.

"We really don't seem to have any values, any absolutes," reflects one. "We've always maneuvered our values to suit our immediate purposes. There is nothing large in our lives."

Discipleship with Jesus frames our life with something large. Discipleship follows the unfolding plan of God for the universe, a project of deep, loving restoration. It's a divine movement of cosmic proportions, a parade of joyful expectation that includes all the stars and planets.

The culture that surrounds us and that breathes into our homes through our TVs and computer screens calls us to something else,

however: it calls us to pursue a career. In fact, the university where I was chaplain for eight years had the motto "Your Career Begins Here!" For our culture, your career, which includes your status and personal security, is of primary importance.

Career comes from a Latin word meaning "race." To pursue a career is to join the race up the ladder—the competition for grades, salaries, and big toys. But as you scramble up the rungs of status and comfort you will surely find heartache and despair. In your quest to avoid suffering, you will certainly find it, most obviously in the form of status anxiety.

The Bible calls this idolatry. Our text in Isaiah pokes fun at this false discipleship. Isaiah says people cut down a tree and use part of the wood for warmth and cooking and then they bow down to the other half in worship and prayer. We do the same, in a way, with our careers: the job that keeps us warm and provides food becomes the sacred center of all our hopes and dreams. It is a very small world.

The school of Jesus offers an alternative to the career race: a holy calling. This calling comes from beyond you and is for the sake of a larger mission. It comes from God the Creator and Redeemer of the world, and its purpose is not to make your life comfortable but to make it a sacrifice of love for that world. The offer is not a ladder but a cross. The Greek word for "witness" is actually *martyr*. Disciples must be ready to die—to ourselves, to our careers.

So whether you are a carpenter, a homemaker, a teacher, or a doctor —you can be a part of this cosmic restoration project. Education, according to this model, is not a passport to privilege or an assurance of safety. It is a quest to learn about the mysteries and wonders of the world in order to sacrificially serve in God's kingdom.

When our careers, our studies, and all of our lives are transformed by the cross, we will experience the deep joy of following God's call.

Talk It Over

1. Isaiah makes idolatry sound absurd. In what ways is careerism just as foolish?

2. What evidence is there in your life that you seek a calling and not only a career?

3. Calling includes much more than your paid work. What else is part of your calling?

In Other Words

"The place God calls you to is the place where your deep gladness and the world's deep hunger meet."

—Frederick Buechner, *Wishful Thinking: A Seeker's ABC*

Do Something!

Play a game like Snakes and Ladders, Monopoly, or The Game of Life. Reflect on the competitive feelings that these games bring out in you and share them with each other.

Cave 23

"There [Elijah] went into a cave and spent the night."
—1 Kings 19:9

*"In the morning, while it was still dark,
[Jesus] got up, left the house and went off
to a solitary place, where he prayed."*
—Mark 1:35

His eyes were wide in fear. His nostrils flared as he tried to catch his breath. Like a deer pursued by hunters, crashing through the woods, he ran for his life. All he heard was the thudding of his heart.

The prophet Elijah had a good reason to be afraid. In a showdown with the false prophets of the pagan religion that dominated the land, God helped him embarrass the rulers of the day, Ahab and Jezebel. An altar, soaked with water, had lit up like a torch when the fire of the Lord fell on it after he prayed. At Elijah's command, nine hundred pagan prophets had been killed by the Israelites. Now it was payback time. Queen Jezebel herself had sent him a message threatening his life: "By this time tomorrow, I will make your life like one of the prophets you had killed."

As he ran south to the relative safety of Judah, God's servant reached the point of total exhaustion. The intense spiritual warfare

of the previous three years had become too much. He fled into the desert, said "Enough!" and promptly fell asleep. The next day, strengthened by an angel, he traveled to Mount Horeb, where he crawled inside a cave. He was totally spent.

None of us have had the experience of battling 900 pagan prophets. On the other hand, we constantly battle a secular culture that majors in noise and minors in agitation. We wrestle with packed schedules, fight with rush-hour traffic, and struggle to meet untold expectations. Disturbing messages buffet us from all sides: panicked radio broadcasts about the latest terrorist attack, insistent e-mails requiring immediate responses, and high-pitched commercials that tell us we don't have enough yet to really be happy. Like Elijah, we find ourselves doing battle with the noise of a pagan religion that promises much but delivers little. The exterior noise of the world we inhabit and the interior noise of our daily lives are so loud that we're ready to pray the prophet's desperate prayer, "I've had enough, Lord!"

Elijah's journey took him from noise to silence. He went from the din of battle and the screams of conflict to the total silence of a cave at the far reaches of a desert. The next day God drew him out of this dark den to the slope of the mountain. There God met his rattled prophet. Not in the noise of the powerful wind, not in the earthquake, nor in the fire did the Lord announce his majestic approach, but in the quiet of a whisper.

In that holy whisper, Elijah heard the two things that he needed to hear: a crucial question and a clarifying answer. God asked him, "What are you doing here, Elijah?" Then God told him what to do and where to go next.

Mark's gospel pictures Jesus' years of ministry as overwhelming, full of demanding expectations and challenging conversations.

His days were filled with the pounding noise of people pleading for help, demons screaming for mercy, and religious leaders shouting "Blasphemy!" So what did Jesus do? At the beginning or the end of every tumultuous day he withdrew to a place of silence where he could "be still" and listen to his Father in heaven.

Every person has the same innate need for silence, for a time of listening and not speaking, for a day of meditating instead of text messaging.

John Cage, a famous avant-garde composer, did an interesting experiment with complete silence when he composed a piece called *4'33"*. At its debut on August 29, 1952, in Woodstock, New York, an audience saw pianist David Tudor raise his piano lid, sit for a while, close and raise his piano lid, sit again for a while, then close the lid and stand up to mark the end of the performance.

The experience of composing and "hearing" *4'33"* led John Cage to conclude that there will always be sound, because in a totally silent recording studio, he still "heard two sounds, one high and one low." The recording engineer attributed the high sound to his nervous system and the low sound to his blood circulation. Christians know that there will always be sound, because the Word of the Lord created and sustains everything, and that Word is always audible to those who have ears to hear.

Perhaps we will never achieve the kind of silence that will let us perfectly hear the Master's voice. But followers of Jesus still do well to regularly follow him to that still, solitary place where our thudding hearts and agitated spirits can settle long enough to hear what the Master wants to whisper to us.

Talk It Over

1. What do you need to disconnect in your life so that you can be more connected to God?

2. Have you ever gone on a silent retreat for one or more days where you spend time thinking, meditating, and praying without speaking to anyone? If so, talk about your experience. If not, would you consider it?

In Other Words

"Silence is the frost heave of the soul. The cold contraction of earth regularly hoists to the surface rocks and stones. Silence has this same habit, lifting subterranean rubble to the surface of our lives that we need to confess and clear out."

—Phil Reinders, *The Banner*, November 2006

Do Something!

Experience five minutes of silence with members of your family or small group. Set a timer and stay in that silent space for the allotted time.

Sam 24

> *"You use steel to sharpen steel,*
> *and one friend sharpens another."*
>
> —**Proverbs 27:17**, *The Message*

> *"This is the very best way to love.*
> *Put your life on the line for your friends."*
>
> —**John 15:13**, *The Message*

The Lord of the Rings by J. R. R. Tolkien is a story about friendship in the midst of a giant struggle. A small band of unrelated people come to defend each other's lives for the sake of the world. Although the dwarf has his mighty axe and the elf his deadly accurate arrows, the most impressive strength of the group is its friendship.

The best picture we have of this is the relationship between the two hobbits, Frodo and his simple but loyal gardener Sam Gamgee. When all the others have been lost to Frodo, Sam remains glued to his side, unshakeable. As the plot gets thicker and darker, and their destination "Mount Doom" gets closer and scarier, Frodo starts to waver and faint.

"I am tired, weary, I haven't any hope left," he moans. A little later he seems defeated: "I never hoped to get across. I can't see any hope of it now." Then he is finished: "Lead me!" he pleads with Sam. "As long as you have any hope left. Mine is gone."

At this point Sam leans into Frodo, and hoists him on his back, carrying him forward one step at a time. More than any other weapon or power, it is friendship that saves the day, and in this story, the world.

Friends hope for each other. Friends carry each other. Friends stick by your side when all else seems lost.

There are many stories of friendship in the Bible. David and Jonathan, Elijah and Elisha, Ruth and Naomi, and of course, Jesus and his disciples. In the same chapter as our text in John, Jesus says to his disciples "I no longer call you servants. . . . I have called you friends" (v. 15). They had hiked many dusty miles together, fed great crowds together, and prayed fervently together. This was more than the formal relationship between staff members.

The purpose of this spiritual friendship was to grow deeper into God's kingdom of love and light. Disciples need this kind of friendship in our lives.

Sometimes that takes a deliberate move on our part. I remember as a campus minister almost falling out my chair one day when a student walked into my office, looked me in the eye and said, "I need to meet weekly with you so my faith can grow." It was a bold and passionate request that doesn't happen too frequently on a secular campus.

As the year went on, we talked about life and learning and even read a book together, chapter by chapter. I realized as we shared and cared for each other that I did not have a similar friend in my own life. I began to pray and look for one.

Over the years, I see how God has gifted me with enduring friends, a marriage partner, and people who I might call my pastor, coach, or mentor. Through their encouragement and wisdom God has strengthened my hope. They have been a Sam to me when the road became dark.

We all need friends, both as peers and as older guides along the way. It has been said that a friend is a mirror, or even a better half, a second self. Friends who help us draw nearer to God and his kingdom are a priceless gift, greater than any treasure of money, technology, or status. So let's pursue the friends we need and nurture the friends we already have.

Talk It Over

1. What are the characteristics of a good friend?

2. Mr. Beaver said of Aslan, in C. S. Lewis's *The Lion, the Witch, and the Wardrobe*: "Safe? . . . 'Course he isn't safe. But he's good." Jesus is a friend, but also our Lord. In what ways is Jesus a friend that is not "safe" but good?

3. The worst thing that can happen in friendship is betrayal. Have you ever been betrayed? Is friendship possible after betrayal?

4. For whom might you be a Sam?

In Other Words

"Walking with a friend in the dark is better than walking alone in the light."

—Helen Keller

Do Something!

Make a card or buy a book and send it to a friend to express your appreciation for their friendship. If that is too sentimental for you, plan an activity like golf and treat him or her to a game.

Empire 25

> *"The Spirit of the Lord is on me, because
> he has anointed me to proclaim good news
> to the poor. He has sent me to proclaim freedom
> for the prisoners and recovery of sight
> for the blind, to set the oppressed free,
> to proclaim the year of the Lord's favor."*
>
> —Luke 4:18 (Isaiah 61:1-2)

While I do not advocate nursing your doubts, I do believe it is good to admit them and engage them. One question that hits me in my faith journey is this: if Jesus is the fulfillment of Isaiah's prophesy, and the year of the Lord's favor has come (the year of Jubilee), why does nothing seem to change in this sad, troubled world? Are the gospels just fables we retell to each other, fooling ourselves into a life of Christ-like service that has never made a lasting difference?

For example, the shock and panic of 9/11 and its aftermath of invasions prompted me to despair. The clouds of dust that hung over New York City left a layer of doubt on my soul: Where is God's empire in a world of terrorism, invasion, and war?

We really need to look at the long stretch of history. In Jesus' time the Roman Empire dominated the world with disciplined military force. But after a few hundred years it grew lax and

eventually was overtaken by another force. Since then there have been numerous empires vying for world power: from the Turks to the Dutch, the Nazis to the Soviets, and from corporate empires to terrorist regimes. The culture of these forces is always highly competitive, and their goal is hostile takeover. When the military is involved, fear and violence become weapons, and these missiles of destruction always circle back. So it is that these empires come and go. And today's empires will suffer the same fate as their predecessors. They will end.

God's kingdom, on the other hand, does not operate that way. It is not manipulated or forced. In the person of Jesus, God demonstrates a kingdom driven not by the love of power but by the power of love. The verse from Luke 4 is part of Jesus' inaugural speech, in which he embraces the marginal and weak. Jesus' kingdom engenders activism that is not interesting to CNN or the daily newspaper. It is a kingdom of compassion that functions mostly under the radar.

Additionally, God's empire does not come about with loud machines and public fanfare but rather through ordinary people. It is implemented by disciples who embrace God's mission through the Spirit and by those who contribute to it even when they do not testify to God's loving empire. God does not coerce, and he works through all people who give themselves up for liberating service.

As human empires come and go, Christ's kingdom lives on. From Saint Paul to Saint Francis to Mother Teresa and Henri Nouwen to you and me, the Spirit of the Lord is upon God's disciples, anointing us to say no to the fear that breeds self-protection and to reach across the gulf of alienation with an open hand of gospel peace. This is a real, lasting empire, and the best one.

Shortly after 9/11 I visited Ground Zero. I saw how a small church right on the edge of the rubble played host to those who worked feverishly to help. Police, firefighters, families of the victims —all found in this church a sanctuary as they tried to piece the world back together again. While the forces of violence are great, the power of hope and love are untiring.

You may doubt this gospel empire at times. Doubts can be the "ants in the pants" of faith, as Frederick Beuchner said. Faith is always stretching out from what is certain to trust in what is not so certain. Is God's kingdom of light and love really real? Ultimately, you can't see this kingdom unless you have the eyes to see it. The Church has not always been faithful to it, and sometimes others have demonstrated it much better. But it is there, and the world is being changed. The question is, how will we live today? To which kingdom will our efforts contribute?

Talk It Over

1. What makes you doubt?

2. What do you do with your doubts?

3. In what ways do you resist, subvert, and challenge the worldly empires around you?

In Other Words

"Jesus . . . was given by the creator God an empire built on love. As we ourselves open our lives to the warmth of that love, we begin to lose our fear; and as we begin to lose our fear, we begin to become people through whom the power of that love can flow out into the world around that so badly needs it."

—N. T. Wright, *Following Jesus*

Do Something!

On some city streets, people stand beside big signs that read "Free Hugs" with arms wide open, ready to give hugs.

You may not be that bold. Instead, why not experiment with the power of a smile by intentionally smiling at a minimum of three strangers in the next twenty-four hours? Report back to your group on the reactions you get.

Snake 26

*"I am sending you out like sheep among wolves.
Therefore be as shrewd as snakes
and as innocent as doves."*
—Matthew 10:16

Being called a sheep is not exactly a compliment. Sheep are walking wool sweaters, if not wolf meat. They are known to be dull, if not dumb. There is a good reason why you have never seen a sign that says "Beware of the Sheep."

Comparing disciples to sheep is a long Jewish tradition—we know this from Psalm 23: "The LORD is my Shepherd, I lack nothing." So Jesus engages his followers with a different analogy: "You must be as shrewd as snakes and as innocent as doves."

The word for *shrewd* here is the same word used in the Septuagint (Greek) version of Genesis 3:1 where it says, "Now the serpent was more *crafty/cunning* than any other wild animal the Lord God had made." Not a comparison you would expect from Christ. What he is pressing home to the disciples is that gullibility will not be enough to live faithfully in a hostile world. In fact, bearing the gospel of peace may take all the inner strength they can muster.

Think like a snake, says Jesus, like a devil if necessary, knowing the mind of the enemy, but not taking on his methods. Be tough-

minded, able to make sharp decisions, incisive in your judgments, worldly wise in your negotiations. Have street smarts. Do all this with a tender heart for the sake of the kingdom of God.

Let's get real: nations struggle for power, promising protection and security to those who conform. Corporations will do anything to capture the souls of children (consumers!) and get them "hooked for life." And there are enough lies in cyberspace to Google you all the way to a cyber hell. Don't be fooled.

If Jesus were to commission us today, he would say we need to be shrewd not only because we may be persecuted but because we may be gradually seduced from our mission. We may become forgetful of the urgency of the gospel call, forgetful of the oppression of those who cry for liberation because some of us just have it *so good*. As the poet Kahlil Gibran said, comfort first comes as a guest to us, then it becomes our host, and eventually, it is our master. It is not that we are being coerced into following a godless emperor, but rather that we are seduced into not caring whether there is an emperor at all.

Discipleship isn't just for sheep. Remember the parable of the Shrewd Manager (Luke 16:1-12). To be all sheep—or all dove—will not suffice in a dog-eat-dog world. Jesus is not suggesting we take on the weapons of the world and get lean and mean, but he is certainly urging us to be fully aware of the hardship that may await those who resist the reigning empire. When he said, "Take up your cross and follow me," it wasn't an invitation to a cakewalk.

Ultimately Christ called us to a dove/snake duality for the sake of love. Different situations will call for different character traits—to become, as the Chinese proverb says, "as hard as the world forces you to be and to be as soft as the world allows you to be." Tender-hearted *and* tough-minded.

John the Baptist said of Christ, "Behold the Lamb of God!" yet Jesus cleared the temple of its buyers and sellers with a whip a few months later. Jesus models a godly character that is not always warm and wooly. It's a tough, enduring, relentless, and determined love that will sacrifice everything to bring this fractured world to wholeness again. Beware of the Lamb.

Be shrewd as a snake and gentle as a dove for the sake of God's kingdom.

Talk It Over

1. Do you tend to think of disciples as pushovers?

2. Can you think of an example in which a Christian may be "shrewd as a snake"?

3. How do you teach children in a world of aggressive marketing to develop snake-like shrewdness without losing their dove-like innocence?

In Other Words

"Never give a man a sword who has not first learned to dance."
—Proverb

Do Something!

As a group, come up with a strategy for handling telemarketers, employment agencies, or high-pressure salespeople. Role-play a scenario together. Be sure to demonstrate dove-like innocence as well as snake-like shrewdness.

Go 27

*"Go out to the roads and country lanes and compel
them to come in, so that my house will be full."*

—Luke 14:23

"Go!" Jesus commanded. Again and again he commanded people to go:
Go to the lost sheep. Go preach the kingdom. Go tell him his fault.
Go and sin no more. Go wash in the pool of Siloam. Go and learn
what this means. Go to the streets and alleys, to the roads and
country lanes. Go sell everything you have and give to the poor.
Go and make disciples of all nations, teaching them all I have
commanded you. Go. Get going. Get out there. Go.

To be honest, I prefer not to go. It is more comfortable to stay in
my comfort zone. But I know that I need to go. If I don't I will never
learn, I will never make a difference, I will never connect with
anyone. The things that need to be done and the people that need
to be seen and the kingdom that needs to be advanced depend on
my willingness to go. Like a soldier in an army, a disciple of Christ
must be willing to go out to do his mission.

It's easier to hear about a lost sheep than to visit someone who
has lost her faith. It's easier to hear a good sermon about God's
kingdom than to tell someone about Christ. It's easier to hold
a grudge than to reconcile with someone who has hurt you. It's
easier to just stay where you are.

But go we must. Jesus said so.

I remember the first time I spoke a Bible-based message in public.
I had to speak to a dozen senile people and their nurses at the local
nursing home. One elderly woman in a wheelchair kept plucking at
my sleeve and saying "Hi, sonny." I kept answering her until my newly-
wed wife whispered that I should ignore her and focus on my message.
I was a wreck. But I had no choice. Because Jesus had said go.

I remember the first time I visited a hospital patient from the church
where I was interning. I didn't know what to say to the other patients
who shared the room or how to create the privacy I needed to
speak pastorally to my parishioner. When a nurse interrupted our
visit I did not dare to ask her to wait. I left without even praying.
My supervisor heard about it and took me to task. I was so insecure.
But I had no choice. Because Jesus had said go.

I remember the first time I went to invite my neighbors to an event
at our church. I wasn't sure what I would say or what kind of reception
I would receive. I stumbled over my words, did my best to make
sure that they felt no pressure at all, and left them the flier with all
the required information. I was so nervous. But I had no choice.
Because Jesus had said go.

I remember the first time I had a tough conversation with someone about her lifestyle. It was the last conversation I wanted to
have. I delayed. I fretted. I put it off some more. Finally I made an
appointment and we met. It was awkward for both of us. There
were moments of silence that hung in the air like blocks of ice,
making the air in the room chilly. I was so scared. But once again,
I had no choice. Because Jesus had said go.

I remember the calls I received to all the churches I've served:
a church in a small town where they set me at the head of the
council table although I had never been an elder before; a campus
ministry at a university where everybody on the faculty had more
impressive academic credentials than I; a church in a midsized
city that met in a gym and counted on growing by reaching out

to the community and offering blended worship; another church that needed healing and also met in a gym, which meant another building program. Each time I did not really want to leave where I was. But what can you do when Jesus says go?

To be a disciple is to go when Jesus tells you to go. Living for Jesus is never static. It is dynamic. It is never easy. It is always challenging.

But here's the thing: when you go, you grow! And good things happen. Not only to others, but also—especially—in you. At the very least, you come home with some beautiful stories, like the seventy-two people Jesus sent out who couldn't stop talking about their experiences on their return.

Ask Christians about their challenging journey as followers of Jesus, and sooner or later you will hear them sheepishly exclaim: "I went because I was sent."

Talk It Over

1. Why is it so hard to go?

2. Where have you gone despite your reluctance and grown because you went where you were sent?

3. Where is Jesus telling you to go right now?

In Other Words

"If exercise was easy, everyone would be doing it."
—Poster in a gym

Do Something!

Play a version of "The Trust Game" in which each person has to fall backwards into someone else's arms. At the signal "Go!" let yourself fall into the unknown and see how it feels.

Stay 28

"How long shall I stay with you and put up with you?"
—Luke 9:41

Are you a frequent mover? In this highly mobile society, chances are great that you are.

Why is this happening? Automobiles, interstate highways, airplanes, and especially the Internet have made us a people who are constantly on the move. With only a click of the mouse at a computer and the flick of a pen on a faxed contract, a person can be transplanted almost instantly to another part of the country, if not the world.

Always going is exciting, but also difficult. In fact, on the Holmes-Rahe Social Readjustment Rating Scale, a change in residence and the accompanying changes in work, school, and church is recognized as extremely stressful. It is not easy to always be saying hello or goodbye.

Is Jesus just another stressful influence with his constant challenges to go? After all, he did tell his disciples that he had "no place to rest his head," and he seemed to suggest that following him meant leaving before burying the dead or saying farewell to the living.

I say "seemed" because I believe that when Jesus says calls us, he often really means stay. Let me illustrate.

Somewhere there is a single mom who wishes that she had the freedom to go out more, travel more, pursue job opportunities in

other parts of the country, and explore new romantic relationships. But her love for her child and her desire to provide long-term stability for her little family makes her stick around. For her, obeying Jesus' call means that she will stay where she is. For the sake of love. Even though she's restless.

Somewhere there is a young couple who are struggling in their marriage. He is wondering what happened to their easy camaraderie; she is wondering why he doesn't understand her need to be heard and to be hugged. But their vows prevent them from leaving and moving out. For them, obeying Jesus' call means that they will stay to work on their relationship. For the sake of love. Even though they're frustrated and upset.

Somewhere there is someone who is disenchanted because a season of discontent has settled on his church. The style of worship, the relevance of the preaching, and the effectiveness of the programs leave a lot to be desired compared to a dynamic church across town. But his commitment to his faith community and his refusal to just consume keeps him coming. For him, obeying Jesus' call means that he will stay and pray through the problems in his home church. For the sake of love. Even though he's disappointed.

Somewhere there is a woman who is grieving the loss of her husband. No, he hasn't died. But a stroke has claimed his memory and he doesn't even know her name anymore. She is lonely and she longs for companionship, especially male companionship. Who would fault her for having an affair even though she is still married! But after a lifetime together, her love for her partner keeps her with him. For her, obeying Jesus' call means that she will stay with him for a while every day, a familiar presence for his confused mind. For the sake of love. Even though she wonders if it makes any difference to him at all.

Mobility and movement are exciting. But they can hurt people and hinder relationships. That's why monastic communities in the Middle

Ages often required not only a vow of chastity or poverty, but also a vow of stability (staying in the same place).

Sometimes a move is necessary and change is welcome. But the one who so often told us to go knew that saving our generation required him to stay and put up with us until he could say, "It is finished."

Let's not overlook the beauty of staying somewhere and going the distance with someone. Let's realize that there are times when go means stay.

Talk It Over

1. How often have you moved in your life?

2. Give an example of someone who decided to stay and endure when things became difficult.

3. Where are you struggling to stay and go the distance?

In Other Words

"Love is neither sentimental or a passing emotion. It is an attraction which gradually becomes a commitment, the recognition of a covenant, of a mutual belonging."

—Jean Vanier, *Commitment and Growth*

Do Something!

Plan a meal or a night out for an individual or family who needs some respite because of a commitment they have made to care for a high-needs person. Have fun surprising them.

Pilgrim 29

"They were transients in this world.
People who live this way make it plain that
they are looking for their true home. . . .
They were after a far better country. . . heaven country."
—Hebrews 11:13-16, *The Message*

Have you ever traveled away from home? Like seeing your home from "Google Earth," it gives you a different perspective on what you've temporarily left.

I took a short-term mission trip to Haiti one year, and it gave me a new perspective on my middle-class suburban life. People lived in small wooden huts; chickens and goats ran freely in the muddy streets; and kids begged for handouts on every corner. The harsh poverty there woke me up to my own privilege and at the same time, my Christian calling.

Our passage today comes from a text that celebrates the faith of the saints. It suggests that they did not feel completely comfortable in their own culture. They saw themselves as transients, as aliens or strangers, or as other translations have it, "pilgrims." Having their eyes set on God's new world, they always saw their home country through the eyes of exiles.

In the Middle Ages, pilgrimage was a common practice for Christians. They would plan a trip to some place that had special significance

for their faith, journeying to the town of a saint like Francis of Assisi or to the Holy Land itself. These Christians would see their trip as a way of being a faithful disciple and growing closer to God.

Some of these pilgrimages degenerated into tourist trips where Christians went to see relics and buy religious trinkets. The Reformers railed against the superstition of it all, and to this day, Reformed Christians have an uneasy relationship with the idea of pilgrimages.

The reality is, we still do it. Some of us go on mission trips, others on tours of special sites in Europe or Israel. I would even suggest that retreats and conferences are like little pilgrimages. All these practices give us pause—time to reflect on our life and get a different perspective, ideally, a more God-centered perspective. We pull ourselves out of the patterns of our popular culture, and this traveling—the physical movement—opens us to a spiritual movement. We become more alert, more attentive, and often more likely to feel a wonder and reverence for the whole of creation. In her book *Practicing Passion,* Kendra Creasy Dean says such pilgrimages can "spiritually dehabituate" us, which means "break us out of old habits, awaken the soul from inertia, renew spiritual energy and insight, and redefine us as people who live 'awed' lives."

I trekked down into the Grand Canyon one summer and camped down there for two nights. At night I went for a hike by myself, and ended up at the edge of a cliff above the Colorado River. I felt I was at the bottom of a gigantic bowl in which the sides rose up slowly all around me and melted into blackness and then stars. I lay down on the rock and stared into the great canopy above, and felt a mix of deep loneliness, wonder, and connection to God all at the same time. Something about the rugged walking, the sweat and fatigue of my journey, seemed to heighten my awareness of who I was and what I needed to become.

Our world belongs to God, but this culture is not our home. A good practice of discipleship can be to take ourselves out of our routines and travel to a place that helps us see ourselves and God's new world more clearly. Not as tourists and sightseers but as true pilgrims seeking to know God's heart for us more intimately. That is our true destiny.

Talk It Over

1. Where have you traveled recently? Was it a tourist trip or did it become a sort of pilgrimage?

2. If you could choose any place to make a pilgrimage, where would it be?

3. Many people take trips to Israel, and some do it as a pilgrimage. How might a trip to Israel have an impact on your faith, if at all?

In Other Words

"The traveler sees what he sees, the tourist sees what he has come to see."

—G. K. Chesterton

Do Something!

Rent a video or DVD from your local store or borrow one from the library together. Choose a foreign film with subtitles and talk with your fellow viewers about how the movie is different from regular Hollywood fare.

Alien 30

*"When an alien resides with you in your land,
you shall not oppress the alien. The alien who resides
with you shall be to you as the citizen among you;
you shall love the alien as yourself,
for you were aliens in the land of Egypt."*

—Leviticus 19:33-34

Here are the Hebrews, running from slavery, wandering through a desert, a great sea of men, women, and children trudging along, looking for a place to call home. They are entering the land of the Canaanites—which includes the Amorites, the Perizzites, the Hivites, and the Jebusites—people who were known to be brutal in their treatment of slaves and animals, and who believed that sexuality was the divine energy that powered the universe. Like television today, it was a culture of sex and violence. Spears were used instead of handshakes.

Leviticus 19 is an expansion on the Ten Commandments. In it Moses tells the Hebrews to be different from the nations around them. Don't mix things up the way they do: don't mate animals of different breeds, don't plant your field with two kinds of seed, and don't wear clothing of two different materials. Yet when it comes to these new neighbors themselves, he says in verse 34, "the alien who resides with you shall be to you as the citizen among you;

you shall love the alien as yourself." Mixing people and races is commanded by God.

In effect, God calls disciples to a double vocation: to have hearts wide open to the foreigner and to be set apart from sinful society.

Too often we live defensively, nurturing a hostility for those who are different. We perpetuate the culture of fear.

Shifting our weight from hostility to hospitality requires more than good intentions. Truly loving our neighbor is more than toleration. Toleration at its best is just putting up with people; at its worst, it becomes indifference. Our text today says, don't just *put up* with the alien in your land, but rather *put them up*. Put them up at your place, in your house. Treat them like your native-born, love them like yourself. Love, as Lewis Smedes described, is a movement toward others without the expectation of reward.

The university is a beautifully diverse yet also disorienting place. As a university chaplain, my job is to play host to many different people: German Lutherans, Polish Catholics, Pakistani Muslims and even the occasional Wiccan, otherwise known as a witch, a true pagan. I remember one Wiccan came by my office worried that the Christians and Muslims on campus, two religions with a history of violence towards pagans, might be hostile toward him. He was asking me if he would be persecuted if he came out of the closet with his faith. I looked at him, this direct descendent of the Canaanites, sitting within my gates. How do we respond?

As I was wandering through Iowa last year I noticed an article in the *Des Moines Register* describing the experience of those who had recently moved into town. The subtitle was "Warm Welcome at Arm's Length." Apparently the aliens felt the locals were friendly enough but kept them at a distance, even after they had lived there for four or five years. If we're honest, we have to admit we can all be just like that. We live in an Arm's Length Society: we choose to be cozy and snug in our own circles.

Disciples, on the other hand are called to form a kind of "Arms Wide Open" society. We risk opening our arms and hearts to the stranger—the immigrant, the person of another race, the neighbor who doesn't share our faith—because Jesus calls us to love our neighbor as ourselves. It's simply the right thing to do.

Think about this. Our text says: "Love the alien as yourself, because you were aliens in Egypt." Love because you know what it's like to be lonely and lost. I know I felt lost at times roaming the big university. I know some people who felt lost as they immigrated to the United States and Canada years ago. And today many disciples feel lost in this post-Christian country.

"You were aliens in the land of Egypt." In other words, do unto others as God has done to you, even if they are enemies. Let gratitude be your guide.

Talk It Over

1. Share with someone else today your own experience: either as "an alien" or as one who was "rescued from Egypt."

2. Hebrews 13 says some have entertained angels unaware. Matthew 24 records Jesus saying "I was a stranger and you invited me in." How have you been surprised and blessed by a guest?

3. Jesus began his life as a refugee in Egypt. How might this guide our attitude toward refugees?

In Other Words

"Our society seems increasingly full of fearful, defensive, aggressive people anxiously clinging to their property and inclined to look at their surrounding world with suspicion, always expecting an enemy to suddenly appear, intrude, and do harm."

—Henri Nouwen

Do Something!

Plan a special meal where you invite people over who are newcomers to town, such as recent immigrants or refugees. If they are able, suggest that they bring a dessert that would be considered part of their homeland cuisine.

Perfume 31

"She has done a beautiful thing to me."
—Matthew 26:10

The other day, a little girl no older than three stood at our door holding out a chocolate bar while her mom hovered a few feet behind her. At age three, she was raising money for an activity sponsored by her preschool. "How much?" we asked.

"Free," she answered innocently, prompting her mom to quickly explain, "No, No. It's $2." Now we happen to believe with Robert Fulghum that you should always "buy lemonade from any kid who is selling." So we bought the chocolate bar and gave to her cause.

In that same week, we were reminded to contribute to the church budget, challenged to buy goats and plows for Third World families, and asked to make a three-year pledge toward a new sanctuary. The mail brought requests from a number of different charities. A college student phoned to ask us to donate to our alma mater. As we walked downtown, a homeless person mumbled, "Got some spare change for a coffee?" It all added up to donation fatigue that forced us to examine our own attitude toward giving. We came up with three worst reasons and three best reasons to give.

The Three Worst Reasons
Don't give because of pressure. Both Moses and Paul insisted on freewill offerings given willingly and cheerfully. There is no blessing in caving in to someone else's pressure tactics or bowing to some-

one else's strong will. Pressured giving usually leads to regret or resentment.

Don't give because of guilt. Guilt is a powerful motivator. Sometimes we need our consciences pricked, but Jesus gave his life to free us from sin and guilt. Our giving is now grounded in gratitude for God's grace.

Don't give because you want to get rid of someone. Limit your giving to causes that mean something to you. Follow up your giving with interest, involvement, and prayer that goes beyond just writing a check. It is OK to say no to charitable causes that have not captured your heart. Don't pay just to make a canvasser go away.

The Three Best Reasons

Do give to worship the Lord. Abel "brought fat portions from some of the firstborn of his flock" (Gen. 4:4). Following his lead, Christ's disciples bring God their very best and trust him to take care of the rest. They manage the Master's money by first giving, then saving, and then living well within their means on what is left. Worship guides them to give their firstfruits, not their leftovers.

Do give to show compassion. Compassion means "suffering with." That's what Jesus did. That's what his disciples do. Genuine care goes beyond feelings of concern and expresses itself in offerings of time, treasures, and talents. How can you tell if the spirit of Jesus truly lives in a person's heart? By her acts of compassion and her charitable giving.

Do give to say thanks. There is no one lovelier than someone who looks for every opportunity to give thanks with a grateful heart. Gratitude moved the newly liberated Israelites to present precious gifts for the building of the tabernacle. Thankfulness motivated the forgiven woman to pour expensive perfume on Jesus' head. Inexpressible appreciation for Christ's willingness to die on the cross for us spurs our own generosity.

Jesus' disciples are joyful givers when they give for all the right reasons: to worship God, to show compassion to those in need, and to express gratitude for the sacrifice that saved them from their sins. Giving for these reasons is sweet perfume to God; it is "doing a beautiful thing" for Jesus.

Talk It Over

1. Talk about a time when you gave because of pressure, guilt, or a desire to get rid of someone. How did that make you feel?

2. Talk about a time when you gave to worship the Lord, show compassion, or express gratitude. How did that make you feel?

3. On a scale of one to ten, how generous would you rate yourself?

4. Tithing is giving 10 percent of your income away. What percentage of your income do you give currently? Do you want to make a change?

In Other Words

"When you have only two pennies left in the world, buy a loaf of bread with one and a lily with the other."

—Chinese proverb

Do Something!

Track all of your income and all of your expenses for the next seven days. Record every penny and closely monitor where your money goes with an eye to finding ways to cut back somewhere and increase your giving.

Or take some five-dollar bills and give them away in the next few days to total strangers you think would benefit from the money.

Desert 32

*"You, God, are my God, earnestly I seek you;
my whole being longs for you, in a dry
and parched land where there is no water."*
—Psalm 63:1

Disciples inevitably hit a desert time, and desert times test your body and spirit.

I spent some time in the stark beauty of Death Valley, California, where the temperature in the blazing sun is 10 degrees Celsius above normal body temperature—48 degrees (about 120 degrees F). Even if you're resting, your body has to work feverishly to keep your temperature down. Without constant gulps of water, you begin to cook. A little headache develops, and your appetite disappears. You dehydrate and feel sick. More than a few have died clawing the sand for water.

Who would want to go to the desert, the place described by the psalmist as "a dry and parched land where there is no water?"

Think of the desert stories of the Bible. The Hebrews spent forty years on the burning sands of the Sinai desert. Moses, Elijah, and Hagar had their most profound experiences of God in the desert. John the Baptist prepared for his ministry in the desert, as did Paul. Finally, our Lord Jesus met Satan most directly in the desert.

The Bible, you might say, is a desert book from a desert people. The desert is always a place of testing and preparing as well as a place of restoration.

So it is with David in our psalm. Most assume the title, "A psalm of David when he was in the Desert of Judah" is a reference to the time he fled the conspiracy to destroy his kingship—led by his own son, Absalom. In other words, David has serious family troubles, he's lost his job, and he is struggling with depression, not to mention a parched mouth. So David flees to a place where no one chooses to go: the desert—"a dry and parched land where there is no water."

Jesus went voluntarily to the desert. David went when he had no other choice. I went just for a vacation, and I can tell you this: if you stop for a moment in the desert, sit down on a rock and gaze at the heat rising from the land, an eerie feeling creeps over you. Nothing moves. Everything is still and absolutely silent. There are no distractions in the desert. No buses barreling past, no car alarms. Not even the buzz of high-voltage wires. Just you, your noisy demons, and God.

The desert may be for you a time of voluntary solitude or perhaps a time of frustration and pain. Feeling *deserted*. The desert has a dark, quiet emptiness that can be frightening. But if you can lay aside all the voices that accuse you and shame you, if you can turn your racing mind down to a gentler pace, you may enter the place of your heart—the place of your will, your dreams, your desires, your hurts, your hopes, your fears. Here too you may find the heart of God. In that moment all illusions die and you can surrender yourself totally to the God who loves you unconditionally.

I believe this was David's experience. He'd lost his job. His family was in shambles. He struggled with his sanity and faith. Yet here in the desert he remembered God's presence as it was so keenly felt in times gone by.

Discipleship neither seeks nor avoids the desert. It weathers the desert to find deeper faith. The desert can pry open our spiritual senses for greater clarity about life. Perhaps even more than in green pastures, it is in the dry desert that we find faith—passionate, totally-dependent-on-God faith.

Talk It Over

1. How can faith grow in a desert in ways that it never could in green pastures?

2. Try to find or imagine a trip to a dry, quiet, or lonely place and listen to your thoughts and prayers as they come. What might God be saying to you?

In Other Words

"You've been leading me
beside strange waters . . .
But where is my pastureland in these dark valleys?"

—Bruce Cockburn, "Strange Waters," *The Charity of Night*

Do Something!

Calculate how much water your household consumes in a day. Include drinking, flushing, washing, and watering the lawn. Then see if you can attempt a 10 percent decrease over the next week as an act of conservation and stewardship.

Gardening 33

*"Applause, everyone. Bravo, bravissimo!
Shout God-songs at the top of your lungs!
God Most High is stunning, astride land and ocean."*

—Psalm 47:1, *The Message*

Faith often seeds and sprouts when we first begin to hear and read about who God is. For many in the Reformed tradition that happens as a child, and faith becomes tightly woven into the routines and ruminations of life. At some point, however, we realize we need *more*. In holy dissatisfaction, we desire to know and love God in deeper or different ways.

In other words, we want the years of head knowledge to sink down through a lump in our throat and make a home in every corner of our heart. One of my college professors, David Benner, describes a spiritual journey like that in his helpful book *Sacred Companions* (IV Press, 2002). He says,

> For many years my knowing of God was primarily a matter of knowing *about* him. Faith was more intellectual assent than emotional reliance or trust, and I related to God much more with my head than my heart. Despite the fact that the Word was made flesh, I tended to turn him back into words—my preferred medium of engagement. . . . Not surprisingly, it resulted in a personal experience of God that was tremendously arid.

At some point, most Christians realize they have been relating to God with just a part of their being. This insight is the beginning of spiritual growth.

Gary Thomas, in his book *Sacred Pathways: Discovering Your Soul's Path to God*, suggests that there are nine "spiritual temperaments," of which *intellectual* is only one. By recognizing there are many other ways to relate to God we might not only be more hesitant to judge those who are different from ourselves but more willing to explore other temperaments throughout the various seasons of our lives.

Here's a quick summary of the other eight temperaments he describes. *Naturalists* are spiritually moved by the wonders of mountains and waterfalls, while *sensates* are drawn to God through the sights, sounds, and smells of life—the glow of stained glass, the harmonies of the choir, or the dry sip of wine at communion. *Caregivers* love God by serving others in need, while *activists* find their participation in God by confronting injustice and unbelief. For the more quiet and introspective seasons of your life, you may find company with the *ascetics,* who strive to live in simplicity, minimizing all distractions, or with the mystical *contemplatives*, who seek to rest in the love of God through prayer and meditation.

Two remain. The *traditionalist* loves God through the stewardship of important Christian rituals and symbols. Finally, the *enthusiast* cheers for God in wonder at all his mysterious ways. I describe the enthusiast last because it appears that the heart of world Christianity today beats with an enthusiast's exuberant rhythm. Most Christians today live in the continents of Africa, Asia, or South America, and they are predisposed to quite naturally cry out with the psalmist, "Bravo, God! Everyone cheer God!"

These temperaments overlap in ways with the gifts of the Spirit, and like them, we do not all receive the same from God. Spiritual maturity comes when we recognize our differences and strive to understand, and even appropriate a little from each type. If you feel like you are in a rut, do not blame your parents or pastor. Seek out brothers and sisters who will show you new ways to connect with God. My college professor may never applaud God in the same way as a Nigerian farmer, but if they met, they might draw each other into a deeper and more holistic experience of God.

Think of your soul as a garden. People typically plant the same vegetables year after year. But most people as they move or change will experiment with different plants and flowers. They may gravitate to their favorites, but maturity as a gardener comes when you know a little bit about how everything grows.

So it is with your spiritual life. The soil is God's Spirit and the sun and water are God's Word, which is the same for everyone. Without them there is no seed, no growth, and no harvest. But the Christian life is full of beautifully rich possibilities. If you feel stuck in an intellectual mode, find friends who will show you how to cheer God. If you are getting weary of all the applause and ache for sound teaching, seek out a mentor. God can touch us in a myriad of ways—we only need to be open to the prompting of his Spirit. Where do you need to grow?

Talk It Over

1. Which of the temperaments discussed here do you most iden-tify with? Which would you like to see more of in your life?

2. In his book David Benner describes a transition from mostly head knowledge to a deep emotional trust in God. How would you describe the ongoing story of your relationship with God?

3. John Calvin called the Psalms "the anatomy of the Christian soul." Which of the nine temperaments do you gravitate to, and which psalm might represent it for you?

In Other Words

"We cannot become what we need to be by remaining what we are."

—Max De Pree, *Leadership Is an Art*

Do Something!

Get a small cup and fill it with soil. Plant a bean seed in the soil and with tender care you may experience the wonder and joy of watching it sprout and grow.

Fish 34

"'Come, follow me,' Jesus said, 'and I will send you out to fish for people. At once they left their nets and followed him."

—Matthew 4:19-20

You might say discipleship grows through stages. For some, it starts with their birth and baptism as an infant. For others, it starts when they embrace the way of Jesus as adults. Either way, people begin to learn the basic disciplines and habits of Christian living. Then they discover their particular gifts and begin to serve in the community with them. When they have demonstrated significant ability and promise, they move into leadership. Finally, as a leader, they begin to develop other leaders.

This whole process, we could say, is "fishing for people."

Sometimes we think fishing is only about getting a new face into church. This is a great act, and it definitely keeps the church colorful and active. But we need to help brothers and sisters discover their gifts, serve as volunteers, and when they are ready, take on a leadership role. This is fishing with a wide net, or you might say, forming a "network" of saints.

Where are you in this process? Who are you encouraging in leadership? Recognize that leadership is not limited to preaching or serving on a board or council. Leadership is taking initiative to make something happen. Some people take initiative to make sure

we celebrate special occasions. Others take initiative to organize, spread the word, and think of the small but important things for such an event. Finally, there are those who lead in cleaning things up after the celebrations are over. All of this is leadership.

Sometimes you are suddenly inspired to service. One campus minister, Graham Morbey, noticed that people on the university campuses appreciated his thoughtful prayers. Then he began to wonder who prays for the professors' research. Research is often risky, cutting-edge, and when published, can be a powerful force of social change. Does it not call for a prayerful process?

So he got some students together and approached a psychology professor about praying for his research. They spent time with the professor, listening to the struggles and issues that lay before him. Carefully and creatively, they composed a prayer for the work entitled "A Prayer for Rudy and His Rats." Seven more prayers for other professors followed. These students who came on board with Graham were being developed as leaders in the area of creative prayer. What a beautiful way to demonstrate Christian discipleship!

Your best leadership abilities will surface when you discover what you are passionate about. Your inspiration and motivation for the work will never dry up because your enthusiasm carries you so naturally forward. To be sure, God does sometimes calls us to leadership experiences we do not like. Moses, Jonah, and Jeremiah are just a few examples. But usually we function best when what we love to do intersects with what people really need.

The disciples loved fishing. Jesus called them to a different sort of fishing. God also calls us to that spiritual fishing.

There is a story of a church that suddenly had eight young people applying for ministry leadership. The church was proud but flabbergasted—they didn't expect so many to arise in a congregation of 225 people. Then an extraordinary theme emerged: all had been approached by the same elderly lady who said, "I think you have the gifts for ministry."

We need to encourage each other towards leadership. That in itself is an act of leadership. Most of us doubt ourselves or are completely unaware of our gifts. We need to fish for those outside the walls of the church *and* for each other. Really, none of us are merely "members" in a church. All are potential ministers.

Talk It Over

1. What leadership skills might you have, or might you grow into?

2. Who in your life has encouraged you to serve in unique ways?

3. How do you intentionally develop the leadership skills you've discovered?

4. Name someone you know whom you could encourage to seek leadership in some way.

In Other Words

"Leadership is muddling through . . . the risk of deciding when the alternatives are equal. . . . It's a relationship of influence . . . it's a serious meddling in other people's lives."

—Walter Wright, *The Mentoring Relationship*

Do Something!

Borrow some kids for an evening. Take them outside to a park and play "Follow the Leader." Take turns playing the leader.

Fool 35

"It is for freedom that Christ has set us free."

—Galatians 5:1

You gotta love garage sales. Old items ignored or forgotten by their owners for years get more attention than a bug in a kid's glass jar. People who would otherwise never drop by to visit jostle each other for the opportunity to park on your lawn. Money that a canvasser couldn't pry from someone's wallet easily exchanges hands. Shy, polite folks who are usually careful to avoid ruffling feathers get into bargaining disputes, going for the thrill of knocking another buck off the asking price.

Think about it. It's a win/win situation. One person is thrilled with some profits and less clutter, the other is delighted by finding the perfect item for the perfect place. One party gets the fun of hosting; the other gets the fun of snooping through other people's stuff. Everybody comes out ahead in the weekend sport of turning trash into treasure.

To raise money for our new building, our church held two huge yard sales. We asked church members for their donations and got enough junk to fill three classrooms and a hallway. There was enough to make a significant dent in the local dump. Truthfully, that's where a lot of it should have gone! But then I reminded myself that God is in the business of transforming old into gold.

As a pastor, I was almost in heaven. One of the things I enjoy about visiting people in their homes is seeing how people live. In fact, people's possessions often give me something to talk about when the conversation becomes a bit stilted. All I have to do is make a comment about a picture on a wall or a carving on a table or a book on a shelf and away we go on a fresh conversational track. Imagine an entire congregation bringing all their conversational fodder to me!

On the actual two Saturdays of the sale, hundreds of people stopped not only to browse but also to buy. A dollar, a quarter, a nickel at a time, all those items were turned into slightly more than two thousand dollars.

Finally, at 3 p.m. as the sale wore on we decided to stop selling and start giving. Everything had to go to make room for our fall programs. Our yard sale organizers came up with a simple strategy. Make a big poster with one word on it: FREE. Then let the pastor make a fool of himself by holding it up at the side of the road. I thought, "Why not? I'm already a fool for Christ!" So for the next two hours I hoisted the sign above my head and smiled for all I was worth.

I was amazed at the power of the word "Free." People slammed on the brakes without thought of following traffic, parking half on the road and half in the ditch. Kids cheered and their parents grimaced when they heard that they could take whatever they wanted. It was amazing. Just when I thought that there were not many treasures left, everything began to disappear. Every now and then someone would hand us a five or a ten over our protests and say, "Here! For your church." Everybody else loved the opportunity to get something for free.

Yeah, you've gotta love garage sales. Especially when you reach the time of the day when it's all about giving and getting for free, when you're glad to be rid of the stuff and someone else is even more glad to take it off your hands.

I had the best time at our yard sale when I stood along the road and held up that beautiful word FREE. In the two hours that I held up that magnetic poster I got more grins and more thanks than a clown giving out animal balloons at a county fair.

Come to think of it, the words "Freedom" and "Free" are the absolutely best words to define our lives as disciples of the one who has "set us free."

Talk It Over

1. Talk about a time when someone gave you something for free.

2. In what ways is a disciple a fool for Christ?

3. What has your freedom in Christ freed you *from*?

4. What does your freedom in Christ free you to do?

In Other Words

"It's all for nothing if you don't have freedom."

—William Wallace, *Braveheart*

Do Something!

Find a number of items in your home that you might put aside for a garage sale. On the next available Saturday morning, display them on a table with the word "Free: Any three items." Have fun chatting with garage salers who stop to browse only to discover that they may choose three things for free. (By setting a limit of three items per person, they will have the challenge of choosing and you will have the fun of being able to repeat this experience with more people.)

Odyssey 36

*"But while [the five foolish virgins] were on their way
to buy the oil, the bridegroom arrived.
The virgins who were ready went in with him
to the wedding banquet. And the door was shut."*
—Matthew 25:10

In 2005, to mark the centennial of the Christian Reformed Church in Canada, 156 cyclists and forty-three support staff traveled all or part of a bicycle tour from Vancouver, British Columbia, to Halifax, Nova Scotia. Ninety-six of those cyclists signed up to go the whole distance: 7,125 kilometers (4,425 miles). They were gone from their families and jobs for more than seventy days. The actual experience of cycling over the mountains, across the prairies, and through the forests while sharing the road with cars, RVs, and transport trucks was hard, exhilarating, and crazy. But when the cyclists dipped their tires into the Atlantic Ocean they were ecstatic. Today, each has an adventure story to tell that rivals the grandest odyssey.

Everyone was invited to join the "Sea to Sea" tour. And many wanted to go. In fact, there were those who, when they saw the different body types and ages of the very ordinary looking participants and observed the tent village and its support vehicles in action, realized with deep regret that they could have gone and should have gone.

So what was the difference between those who went and those who stayed behind? A decision.

People used to sing at evangelistic crusades *"I have decided to follow Jesus."* The song recognized that a life of discipleship, like a summer on a bicycle, begins with a decision.

The decision for my marriage partner and me to cycle across Canada with the tour affected everything we did for the next two years. We trained, saved money for new bicycles and gear, accumulated vacation time, and raised funds. It was the same for every other cyclist. As a result, when everyone gathered for orientation at the University of British Columbia on June 22, all of us were ready. Like the five young women in Jesus' parable who decided to go to the wedding and followed that up with the wise decision to take extra fuel for their oil lamps, every cyclist was prepared to go "Sea to Sea." What set these cyclists apart was one big decision to participate and a thousand daily decisions in support of that initial decision. As I experienced firsthand that unforgettable summer of celebration and saw the positive impact that the tour had on the church, on the communities through which we cycled, and especially on the participants, I often thought, "What a difference a decision makes!"

Christian discipleship can be seen as one big decision to respond affirmatively to God's saving work followed by many smaller, daily decisions that celebrate and reflect Christ's beautiful life. It begins with God first and always saying yes to us; it continues with us saying yes back to God again and again.

Recently I met with some folks who had signed up for a discipleship course. On this particular night we were faced with the challenge to set aside a daily quiet time to meditate on God's Word. Everyone in the room had already made the big decision to follow Jesus.

Everyone had also decided to study Greg Ogden's book, *Discipleship Essentials* with me. Now it was time to make another decision related to our life in Christ.

"So," I asked, looking around. "Have you decided when and where you will have your daily rendezvous with the Lord?" One by one the participants made their decision known. "In the afternoon in my living room when my child is napping," said a young mom. "In my pickup truck at lunchtime," said a construction worker. "I will commute to the city twenty minutes earlier and take my quiet time in my favorite coffee shop before I start work," said another man who had struggled to find any time at all.

The bridegroom is coming again. He invites you on an odyssey that will climax in a feast that you do not want to miss. What a difference every decision you make will have on that celebration!

Talk It Over

1. What decisions do you need to make to join or continue the most important celebration of all?

2. In our Reformed covenant theology we stress that God chooses us before we choose God. Why is it still vitally important to respond to God's yes with our own yes?

In Other Words

"If God did not choose us first, he'd have no children besides Jesus. Therefore God takes the first step. He brings his saving work into our lives to make us willing and able to respond to him."

—Robert De Moor, *Quest of Faith,* Faith Alive Christian Resources

Do Something!

Light an oil lamp or a candle and turn off every light in the room. Let the tiny flame be a symbol of confidentiality. In the intimacy of the flame's soft glow, have every member of your family or small group take a turn mentioning one thing that requires a decision right now. Conclude by having each one say a brief prayer for the person sitting to the left, asking God to help him or her with the deciding process and to find peace with the final decision.

Wind 37

> "Suddenly a sound like the blowing of
> a violent wind came from heaven and filled
> the whole house where they were sitting."
>
> —Acts 2:2

Many factors had a bearing on the Sea to Sea cyclists' daily ride as they cycled across Canada in 2005: temperature, terrain, diet, bike maintenance, general health, and the previous day's effort. But nothing affected them more than the wind. Its direction and speed always made all the difference!

Your authors had the privilege of doing the entire distance and serving as co-chaplains on the tour. When we were done, people wanted to know which days were the hardest. We did not have to think long about the answer: July 15 when we cycled from Gull Lake to Chaplin, Saskatchewan, and July 23 when we cycled from Portage La Prairie to Winnipeg, Manitoba. People also asked us about our best days. That too was easily answered: July 9 when we soared from Canmore to Calgary, Alberta, at top speed and September 3, the final day, when we raced from Truro to our final destination, Halifax, Nova Scotia.

Now here's the interesting thing. We have seen photographs of each of these days. Just from looking at the pictures, all you would think is, "What wonderful terrain! What a beautiful day for riding."

That's because the most important factor making it either our worst day or our best day was *invisible*, that unseen force called the wind. Cycling across Canada taught us that biking into a relentless headwind all day long can really beat you down, while riding at breathtaking speeds with a powerful tail wind at your back is an absolute thrill.

On Pentecost, the Holy Spirit announced his arrival with the sound of a "violent wind" (TNIV), as a "gale force" (*The Message*). Why was the Spirit revealed in this way? Perhaps to let us know that, like the wind, the Spirit is a fierce friend we want behind us, not against us.

Here's the thing. The Spirit wants to be at your back, propelling you forward in the direction God wants you to go. In fact, you definitely need the Spirit behind you as an empowering tail wind, especially when you are faced with a mountain of worry, a hot day of frustration, or a valley of grief. And the best way to put him there is to follow Jesus and live the life of a disciple who obeys the Master's orders, especially the beautiful command to love one another as he first loved us.

Here's the other thing about the Holy Spirit. If, like the prophet Jonah, you choose to head off in a direction that God does not want you to go, the Spirit will be in your face like a demoralizing headwind, trying to prevent you from going in the wrong direction. In fact, anything that is *unholy* in your life will prompt the *Holy* Spirit to become a relentless gale force in your face until, like a weathervane submitting to the wind, you repent and turn in God's direction.

When the Sea to Sea tour was first proposed, it was suggested that we cycle from Halifax to Vancouver. One of the earliest and wisest decisions tour organizers made was to change directions and cycle from British Columbia to the Maritimes. They recognized that the prevailing winds blow from west to east; they also understood that working with the prevailing winds would provide the cyclists the best chance of making it all the way across the country. For the most part, with a few exceptions like those two tough days in the prairies, it worked that way.

Welcome the work of the third person of the Trinity in your life. And remember this: your fierce friend, that violent wind we know as the Holy Spirit, will blow the breath of God in your face until you bend and turn and follow Jesus. So you might as well bend to the Master's beautiful will sooner rather than later and get all the divine support you'll need for your journey.

Talk It Over

1. It has been said that a flag is the wind made visible. In what ways is a Christian the Holy Spirit made visible?

2. Which way is the Spirit wind blowing in your life right now?

3. How open are you to the leading of the Holy Spirit?

In Other Words

May the road rise up to meet you.
May the wind be always at your back.
May the sun shine warm upon your face;
the rains fall soft upon your fields and until we meet again,
may God hold you in the palm of his hand.

—Traditional Gaelic blessing

Do Something!

Have everyone in your family or small group make a pinwheel out of paper. You will need paper, scissors, a pin, and a stick. Experiment with making it spin by blowing air at it or running with it.